Thoughts
from a
Warmed
Heart

In the evening I went very unwillingly to a society in Aldersgate-Street, where one was reading Luther's preface to the Epistle to the Romans. About a quarter before nine, while he was describing the change which God works in the heart through faith in Christ, I felt my heart strangely warmed. I felt I did trust in Christ, Christ alone for salvation: And an assurance was given me, that he had taken away *my* sins, even *mine*, and saved *me* from the law of sin and death.

Wesley's *Journal*,
24 May 1738

Thoughts
from a
Warmed
Heart

A commentary on
John Wesley's Notes
on the New Testament

James T MacCormack

COLOURPOINT

6 5 4 3 2 1

© JT MacCormack
2002

Designed by Colourpoint Books,
Newtownards
Printed by W & G Baird Ltd

ISBN 1 898392 28 5

Colourpoint Books
Unit D5, Ards Business Centre
Jubilee Road
NEWTOWNARDS
County Down
Northern Ireland
BT23 4YH
Tel: 028 9182 0505
Fax: 028 9182 1900
E-mail: info@colourpoint.co.uk
Web-site: www.colourpoint.co.uk

About the Author

James T MacCormack was born in Dublin in 1926. He was educated at Wesley College and the University of Dublin (TCD) from which he graduated with a BA in 1948. He received his BD four years later. Jim was ordained as a Methodist minister in January 1954, while working for the church in Northern Rhodesia (now Zambia). During his time in Africa (roughly a third of his career), he became an expert translator, including working on a revision of the Tonga Bible under the auspices of the Bible Society. On returning to Ireland in 1971 he ministered in Seymour Hill and Whitehead, and served as Senior Tutor at Edgehill Theological College where, among other subjects, he lectured on Wesley's *Notes on the New Testament.* Since retirement in 1994, Jim has lectured occasionally and been occupied with this important project.

The Veterans are at work.

Contents

Abbreviations

AV	Authorised Version (1611)
GNB	Good News Bible (1978)
JB	Jerusalem Bible (1966)
NIV	New International Version (1980)
New RSV	New Revised Standard Version (1989)
REB	Revised English Bible (1989)
EV	English Version
EVV	English Versions
LXX	Greek translation of the Hebrew Bible, from which the NT writers quoted. It was made by 70 (possibly 72) translators. Hence the name Septuagint and the abbreviation.

Use of italics

In keeping with the style of the early editions of Wesley's *Explanatory Notes upon The New Testament*, all passages quoted directly from the Bible, within quotations from the *Notes,* appear in italics.

Introduction

Methodist doctrines according to
Wesley's Notes on the New Testament

IN 1955, EPWORTH PRESS PUBLISHED *Selections from Wesley's
Notes on the New Testament* by John Lawson. The Reverend
John Lawson became a lecturer in a Methodist seminary of the
United Methodist Church in the United States of America. When
training to be a Local Preacher, he found himself confronted
with the requirement to read Wesley's *Notes* on the New
Testament. "This requirement was conscientiously fulfilled,
without any immediate profit to the reader." Lawson hoped that
his *Selections* would help Methodist preachers to appreciate
parts of the *Notes* and so be encouraged to read the whole.

ush.' That book has been out of print for many years. However,
Reverend Lawson made available to me much of his further
work on the *Notes*, research which he had done in preparation for
the volume on the *Notes* to appear in the Abingdon edition of
Wesley's *Works*. *J.L is Now over 90!*

To read the *Notes* with profit meets with three difficulties:
firstly, the print is very small; secondly, many of the explanations
are unnecessary at the start of the twenty-first century; and
finally, any particular doctrine is to be found only by compiling
notes on many verses. Lawson's *Selections*, and now this book,
remove these three difficulties. Wesley's acknowledgement in
the preface of his indebtedness to four writers prompts the idea
that the *Notes* are not as fully Wesley's work as the *Sermons* are.
Thus they appear to be inferior. However, developing Lawson's
work, and by analysing Matthew chapters 1–7, John chapters
1–8, Hebrews chapters 1–7, and Jude, I found that 39 per cent of
the *Notes* are attributable to the four named sources. Thus, 61 per
cent are Wesley's own work. In some notes, Wesley can be very
independent: his notes on Romans chapter 3:23–6 are 80 per
cent his own.

Wesley's own estimation of the value of the *Notes* is very high, and his directions to his preachers and societies concerning their use are clear. Indeed, he wrote them for all who have "a desire to save their souls". From the moment of publication, preachers were directed to the *Notes*. The first and second editions were quarto volumes. But the third was duodecimo for the convenience of itinerant preachers who carried them in their saddlebags. Wesley ordered his preachers to read frequently and enlarge upon a portion of the *Notes* in public. The third edition was the result of a revision made by John and Charles Wesley and several others "carefully comparing the translation with the original and correcting or enlarging the *Notes* as we saw occasion". In the *Journal*, Wesley records a revision of the *Notes* as late as December 1787. Five editions and the careful attention given to the translation of the Greek, as well as the *Notes* themselves, show the importance which they had for Wesley, and through him for the "preachers in connexion with Mr. Wesley". The minutes of the Methodist Conference of 1776 record in detail the examination of William Ellis for admission as a preacher. Among the questions asked is: "Have you read the *Sermons* and the *Notes on the New Testament*?" These questions were put to all before they were admitted as preachers.

The *Notes* became one of Methodism's standards of doctrine in 1763, when Wesley published a pamphlet known as the *Large Minutes*. This contained a form of trust deed, designed as a model upon which the trust deeds of Methodist property were to be drawn. A clause of this model deed provided that the preachers should preach "no other doctrine than is contained in Mr. Wesley's *Notes on the New Testament* and the four Volumes of *Sermons*". To this day the *Notes* and the *Sermons* (now 44 in one volume) are the standards for Methodist preachers: "The doctrines of the evangelical faith which Methodism has held from the beginning and still holds are based upon the divine revelation recorded in the Holy Scriptures" (Constitution of the Methodist Church in Ireland). *Notes upon the New Testament*, which is the record of the evangel, have a natural place in such a constitution.

8

1
Scripture

WESLEY PROCLAIMS HIS RESPECT FOR the Bible both in the preface to the *Sermons* (paragraph 5) and in the preface to the *Notes* (paragraph 3). He writes these "for plain, unlettered men, who understand only their mother tongue and yet reverence and love the Word of God and have a desire to save their souls". Wesley had the same love and reverence for Scripture. He felt that the Bible could bring all Christians together, so powerful and central is it, as he writes at paragraph 9:

> Would to God that all the party names and unscriptural phrases and forms which have divided the Christian world were forgot, and that we might all agree to sit down together, as humble, loving disciples, at the feet of our common Master, to hear His word, to imbibe His Spirit, and to transcribe His life in our own!

Out of this respect for the Bible, Wesley seeks to reconcile differences in the accounts of the same event: see the *Notes* for Luke 6:20; 22:58; and 23:34; and also the preface (paragraph 6).

Wesley shows this respect for Scripture in the very first note for Matthew 1:1:

> If there were any difficulties in this genealogy, or that given by St. Luke, which could not easily be removed, they would rather affect the Jewish tables than the credit of the evangelists; for they act only as historians, setting down these genealogies as they stood in those public and allowed records. Therefore they were to take them as they found them. Nor was it needful they should correct the mistakes, if there were any. For these accounts sufficiently answer the end for which they are recited. They unquestionably prove the grand point in view, that Jesus was of the family from which the promised Seed was to come. And they had more weight with the Jews for this purpose than if alterations had been made by inspiration itself. For such

alterations would have occasioned endless disputes between them and the disciples of our Lord.

Wesley uses the same approach to account for the difference between the quotation at Hebrews 2:7 – "a little lower than the angels" – and the original in Psalm 8:5 – "a little lower than God/a god" – as the Hebrew of Psalm 8 could be translated. The word "angels" comes from the Septuagint, the version commonly used by Greek-speaking Jews.

His respect for Scripture is again seen at the following notes:

In words taught by the Holy Spirit – Such are all the words of Scripture. How high a regard ought we, then, to retain for them![1 Corinthians 2:13]

Give thyself to reading – Both publicly and privately. [1 Timothy 4:13]

Wesley is referring to the reading of Scripture; there is no other book, which he read "publicly and privately".

Similar notes are found at 1 John 4:1; preface to Revelation; and Revelation 1:1–3; 22:18–19.

The Inspiration of Scripture

(a) Its Purpose

Wesley sets forth at Matthew 1:1 a guide for the interpretation of any passage of Scripture – "the end for which it was written". He also accepts that Scripture may be limited by the knowledge of any particular time. Inspiration, should it correct human knowledge, may not always be helpful. And so errors – in this case in the genealogies – may remain uncorrected. The purpose for which any verse is written is all-important. Wesley puts this guide into practice at 2 Timothy 3:16:

All scripture is inspired of God – The Spirit of God not only once inspired those who wrote it, but continually inspires, supernaturally assists, those that read it with earnest prayer.

Hence it is so *profitable for doctrine*, for instruction of the ignorant, *for* the *reproof* or conviction of them that are in error or sin, *for* the *correction* or amendment of whatever is amiss, and for instructing or training up the children of God *in* all *righteousness*.

The note highlights the purposes for which Wesley believes Scripture is inspired. Further, the Spirit's help to the reader is essential for understanding.

(b) Its Extent

See the note on 1 Corinthians 2:13 (above).

For Paul, Scripture was the Law, the Prophets and the Writings. The note on 1 Corinthians 7:25 claims the same inspiration for the writings of the Apostles.

I have no commandment from the Lord – By a particular revelation. Nor was it necessary that he should; for the apostles wrote nothing that was not divinely inspired: but with this difference – sometimes they had a particular revelation, and a special commandment; at other times they wrote from the divine light which abode with them, the standing treasure of the Spirit of God. And this, also, was not their private opinion, but a divine rule of faith and practice. *As one* whom God hath made *faithful* in my apostolic office; who therefore faithfully deliver what I receive from Him.

A similar note is found at 1 Corinthians 7:40. See also 2 Corinthians 11:17, Galatians 3:8, and the preface, paragraphs 10 and 12.

(c) Its Nature

(i) Inspiration sometimes is by dictation:

They parted my garments among them – No circumstance of David's life bore any resemblance to this, or to several other passages in the twenty-second Psalm. So that in this scripture, as in some others, the prophet seems to have been thrown into a preternatural ecstasy, wherein, personating the Messiah, he barely spoke what the Spirit dictated, without any regard to himself. [John 19:24]

A similar note is found at 2 Peter 1:21.

(ii) Inspiration sometimes is by special revelation:

I received [from the Lord] – By an immediate revelation. [1 Corinthians 11:23]

See also 1 Corinthians 7:25 (above).

(iii) Inspiration does not eclipse personality:

For the spirits of the prophets are subject to the prophets – But what enthusiast considers this? The impulses of the Holy Spirit, even in men really inspired, so suit themselves to their rational faculties, as not to divest them of the government of themselves, like the heathen priests under their diabolical possessions. Evil spirits threw their prophets into such ungovernable ecstasies, as forced them to speak and act like madmen. But the Spirit of God left His prophets the clear use of their judgement, when, and how long, it was fit for them to speak, and never hurried them into any improprieties either as to the matter, manner, or time of their speaking. [1 Corinthians 14:32]

After much debate – It does not appear that this was among the apostles themselves. But if it had, if they themselves had debated at first, yet might their final decision be from an unerring direction. For how really soever they were inspired, we need not suppose their inspiration was always so instantaneous and express as to supersede any deliberation in their own minds, or any consultation with each other. [Acts 15:7]

(iv) Inspiration is not always literal – in the sense of word for word exactness:

Thou art in no wise the least among the princes of Judah . . .

When this and several other quotations from the Old Testament are compared with the original, it plainly appears the apostles did not always think it necessary exactly to transcribe the passage they cited, but contented themselves with giving the general sense, though with some diversity of language. [Matthew 2:6]

See also Matthew 1:8 (quoted above); 2:15; and Hebrews 1:5.

(v) Inspiration is not always literal – in the sense of fact or act corresponding to the ordinary meaning of the words:

Ye ought also to wash one another's feet – And why did they not? Why do we not read of any apostle washing the feet of any other? Because they understood their Lord better. They knew He never designed that this should be literally taken. He designed to teach them the great lesson of humble love, as well as to confer inward purity upon them. And hereby He teaches us (1) in every possible way to assist each other in attaining that purity; (2) to wash each other's feet, by performing all sorts of good offices to each other, even those of the lowest kind, when opportunity serves, and the necessity of any calls for them. [John 13:14]

See also Matthew 5:40–1 (Wesley's note is peculiar in that he does not quote any of the phrases of these two verses): "The meaning of the whole passage", ie verses 39–41. The final sentence of the note refers to the phrase "turn the other cheek". Our Lord did not do this at John 18:22–3. The same applies very explicitly at Revelation 5:1.

In the notes referring to inspiration, Wesley uses reason to interpret the New Testament. Reason is a tool for interpretation:

But in understanding be ye grown men – Knowing that religion was not designed to destroy any of our natural faculties, but to exalt and improve them, our reason in particular. [1 Corinthians 14:20]

This correlation between the inspiration of the Holy Spirit and the rational faculty of people is applied to the problem created by the 'enthusiasts' of the eighteenth century:

> Evil spirits . . . forced them [their prophets] to speak and act like madmen. But the Spirit of God left His prophets the clear use of their judgement, when, and how long, it was fit for them to speak, and never hurried them into any improprieties either as to the matter, manner, or time of their speaking. [1 Corinthians 14:32]

> *Paul was pressed in spirit* . . . Every Christian ought diligently to observe any such pressure in his own spirit, and . . . if he does not, he will feel great heaviness. [Acts 18:5]

See also the note at John 3:31 – here Wesley uses his reason to decide who is speaking. The New RSV, GNB and REB all follow him. See also the notes at John 13:14 and Revelation 5:1.

The use of reason to interpret Scripture is required by the very nature of Scripture itself. Concerning the Sermon on the Mount, Wesley comments:

> Through this whole discourse, we cannot but observe the most exact method which can possibly be conceived. Every paragraph, every sentence, is closely connected both with that which precedes and that which follows it. And is not this the pattern for every Christian Preacher? If any then are able to follow it without any premeditation, well; if not, let them not dare to preach without it. No rhapsody, no incoherency, whether the things spoken be true or false, comes of the Spirit of Christ. [Matthew 5:9]

Wesley sees this rational coherency – "an exactly regular series of arguments" – in every book of the New Testament (preface, paragraph 11).

However, reason alone is not sufficient for the interpretation of Scripture. Wesley knew this by his experience of spiritual distress, despite having followed the Christian way with all his rational powers:

> *The things of the Spirit* – The things revealed by the Spirit of
> God, whether relating to His nature or His kingdom – *For they
> are foolishness to him* [the natural man] – He is so far from
> understanding, that he utterly despises them. *Neither can he
> know them* – As he has not the will, so neither has he the power.
> *Because they are spiritually discerned* . . . by the aid of that
> Spirit, and by those spiritual senses, which he has not. [1
> Corinthians 2:14]

> *For the Spirit searcheth even the deep things of God* – Be they
> ever so hidden and mysterious; the depths both of His nature and
> His kingdom. [1 Corinthians 2:10]

The notes on 1 Corinthians 2:10 are all relevant to this
inadequacy of reason by itself.

Even with the help of the Holy Spirit, Wesley feels that parts
of the Scripture are beyond our powers of understanding, and so
we must read all of it with humility. He confesses his utter
despair of understanding parts of Revelation (see his preface to
the book of Revelation). Bengel's commentary on Revelation,
he writes, "revived my hope of understanding even the
prophecies of this book; at least some of them: for perhaps
some will not be opened for an eternity".

For a true understanding of Scripture, the correct text must be
established. By Wesley's estimation, the best English version
available was the Authorised.

> Yet I do not say it is incapable of being brought, in several
> places, nearer to the original. Neither will I affirm that the
> Greek copies from which this translation was made are always
> the most correct; and therefore I shall take the liberty, as
> occasion may require, to make here and there a small alteration.
> [preface, paragraph 4)

In the next paragraph Wesley seeks to answer those who say
"the text is altered too much and others that it is altered too

little". He feels that there is something, "I know not what peculiarly solemn and venerable in the old language of our translation". He desires to keep "the very words by which God has often conveyed strength or comfort to our souls" (preface, paragraph 5). Nevertheless, where "the sense was made better, stronger, clearer or more consistent with the context" or "nearer the original", he made alterations – about four thousand! Some of these anticipate current translations.

> . . . *strain out a gnat* . . . It is strange, that glaring false print, 'strain at a gnat,' which quite alters the sense, should run through all editions of our English Bibles. [Matthew 23:24]

Wesley alters "blessed" to "happy" at Matthew 5:3 ff, and "charity" to "love" at 1 Corinthians 13. He omits the name Paul from the title of "the Letter to the Hebrews" even though he argues that the author was indeed Paul (preface to this letter).

One of Wesley's major alterations occurs at 1 John 5:7–8; he transposes these verses. His justification for this "small alteration" is as follows:

> What Bengelius has advanced, both concerning the transposition of these two verses, and the authority of the controverted verse, partly in his *Gnomon*, and partly in his *Apparaticus Criticus*, will abundantly satisfy any impartial person. [1 John 5:7]

Wesley corrects the text of the AV, so respected by him and his people, without omitting any words of that version. Such excision would not have helped the plain unlettered man on his way to heaven. Nevertheless, his alteration shows his desire to find the best text and the best translation.

The *Notes on the New Testament*, from the first edition to the present, reprints the text, the AV with Wesley's emendations, at the top of each page. The print is the same size as appears in many editions of the Bible today. The notes are in smaller print on the lower part of each page. This is not a matter of printing

– it is a matter of principle, "that the comment may not obscure or swallow up the text" (preface, paragraph 6). All that one needs to know of God is contained in the Bible, and especially in the New Testament. The clear division in the *Notes*, even though this requires Wesley to repeat, in his note on each verse, the phrases of that verse, emphasises the supremacy of Scripture for this preacher – and for those "in connexion" with him.

The supremacy of Scripture and respect for it, the desire to find the original text, the four-strand understanding of inspiration derived from Scripture itself, and the place of reason vis-à-vis inspiration – all these are very relevant to our interpretation and proclamation of the Gospel today.

2
Doctrine of God

THE NEW TESTAMENT IS THE Good News of Jesus and the Good News which is Jesus. The books of the New Testament are the "words of the most gentle and benevolent Jesus" (preface, paragraph 9). Thus Wesley's doctrine of God (in the sense of the first person of the Trinity) appears within the framework of the New Covenant of our Lord and Saviour Jesus Christ. This is a blessing because, although the revelation given through Abraham, Moses and the prophets was authentic, the writer of the fourth Gospel declares firmly that, "No man hath seen God at any time; [Jesus] who is in the bosom of the Father, he hath declared him" (John 1:18). Wesley comments: "The expression denotes the highest unity, and the most intimate knowledge." Thus, in the *Notes* we find the doctrine of God as it appears in the light of Jesus, the Word of God. The note at John 14:10 derives from this "highest unity and most intimate knowledge": "*I am in the Father*. The words that I speak . . . I am one with the Father in essence, in speaking, and in acting."

In contrast to the birth narratives of Matthew and Luke, the fourth Gospel sets the incarnation in the context of the eternal God. Hence John 1:1 gives Wesley the opportunity to affirm his orthodoxy concerning this doctrine: "Jesus . . . is *the Word* . . . by whom the Father speaking maketh all things".

God is the sole creator. Wesley surmises at John 1:1 that John the writer is concerned to show that Jesus is truly God: "But when at length some from hence began to doubt His Godhead, then St. John expressly asserted it". Thus when Wesley describes Jesus "as supreme, eternal, independent", these are the attributes which he understands God to have. At John 4:24 he comments: "*God is a Spirit* – Not only remote from the body . . . full of all spiritual perfections, power, wisdom, love, holiness."

These and other attributes are ascribed to God at Revelation 1:8:

> *I am the Alpha and the Omega, saith the Lord God* . . . God is the beginning, as He is the Author and Creator of all things, and as He proposes, declares, and promises so great things: He is the end, as He brings all things which are here revealed to a complete and glorious conclusion.

Wesley assesses the description of God *"who was, and . . . who is to come"* as "A wonderful translation of the great name JEHOVAH" (Revelation 1:4). God who is named in the New Testament is most certainly the God of Abraham, Isaac and Jacob and the God of Moses (Cf Exodus 3:13–16).

Revelation, Chapter 4, is a vision of God on the throne with four living creatures proclaiming Him to be "Holy, holy, holy":

> This word properly signifies *separated* . . . And when God is termed holy, it denotes that excellence which is altogether peculiar to Himself . . . the glory flowing from all His attributes conjoined . . . whereby He is, and eternally remains, in an incomprehensible manner separate and at a distance, not only from all that is impure, but likewise from all that is created.
> God is separate from all things. He is, and works from Himself, out of Himself, in Himself, through Himself, for Himself. Therefore, He is the first and the last, the only One and the Eternal, living and happy, endless and unchangeable, almighty, omniscient, wise and true, just and faithful, gracious and merciful. [verse 8]

This is a useful but incomplete summary of Wesley's understanding of God. It may be justified by two factors: (i) The ten attributes "the first and the last, the Only One . . . omniscient" belong to God by definition; (ii) Verse 3 describes God through the medium of colour:

> If there is anything emblematical in the colours of these stones, possibly the *jasper*, which is transparent and of a glittering

white, with an intermixture of beautiful colours, may be a symbol of God's purity, with various other perfections, which shine in all His dispensations. The *sardine stone*, of a blood-red colour, may be an emblem of His justice . . . *An emerald*, being green, may betoken favour to the good . . . the everlasting covenant. See Gen. ix 9.

This symbolical interpretation of the colours accounts for the remaining three pairs of attributes at verse 8.

It is worth reading Revelation 4:8–11 complete with Wesley's notes thereon. He concludes:

It is to the free, gracious, and powerfully working will of Him who cannot possibly need anything that all things owe their first existence . . . [and] continue in being ever since they were created.

See also Acts 17:26, 28 and 1 Corinthians 10:36.

Wise and True

But wisdom is justified by all her children – The children of wisdom are those who are truly wise – wise unto salvation. The wisdom of God in all . . . these various methods of calling sinners to repentance, is owned and heartily approved by all these. [Luke 7:35]

O the depth of the riches, and wisdom, and knowledge of God! . . . the *depth of the riches* is described, verse 35; the *depth of wisdom*, verse 34; the *depth of knowledge*, in the latter part of this verse. *Wisdom* directs all things to the best end; *knowledge sees* that end. [Romans 12:33]

For since, in the wisdom of God – According to His wise disposals, leaving them to make the trial. *The world* – Whether Jewish or Gentile, *by* all its boasted *wisdom knew not God* – Though the whole creation declared its Creator, and though He declared Himself by all the prophets; *it pleased God, by* a way which those who perish count mere *foolishness, to save them that believe.* [1 Corinthians 1:21]

Out of [God's] free grace and mercy. *Are ye –* Engrafted *into Christ Jesus, who is made unto us* that believe *wisdom,* who were before utterly foolish and ignorant. [1 Corinthians 1:30]

These four notes demonstrate clearly that Wesley is concerned first and last with the good news of Jesus, Saviour of the world. These are *Explanatory Notes on the New Testament,* the New Covenant offered by God to people. Hence, notes on God's wisdom are limited, mostly, to His work of reconciling people to Himself. See also Ephesians 1:8. We may contrast Wesley's note on 1 Corinthians 1:22: " . . . *and the Greeks,* or Gentiles, *seek wisdom –* The depths of philosophy, and the charms of eloquence".

Wesley acknowledges the place of natural theology at Acts 17:28 and also at Romans 1:19, 21. But the wisdom of the Greeks makes them regard *"Christ crucified"* as *"foolishness –* A silly tale, just opposite to the *wisdom* they seek" (I Corinthians 1:23). He goes on to comment at I Corinthians 1:24:

But to them who are called – And obey the heavenly calling. *Christ –* With His cross, His death. His life, His kingdom. And they experience, first, that He is *the power,* then, that He is *the wisdom, of God.*

The experience of reconciliation is proof of the wisdom of God. Wesley had kept the commandments of God, and the ordinances of the Church. Neither had given assurance and joy in his relationship with God. These came out of his experiences of 24 May 1738. This experience – "being engrafted into Christ Jesus" – opens to all people the doors to "wisdom, and righteousness, and sanctification, and redemption". Redemption is "complete deliverance from all evil, and eternal bliss" (1 Corinthians 1:20–31). This is the content of the wisdom of God in the New Testament, in Wesley's mind. (See also Ephesians 1:17.)

Revelation 5:12 and 7:12 refer to wisdom in a wider sense, namely God's governance of the world. However, these verses occur in the context of the proclamation of the salvation which the Lamb (the crucified Saviour) has accomplished and so the notes thereon refer to wisdom in this sense.

The "manifold wisdom of God", according to Paul, is "made known by the church" (Ephesians 3:10). Wesley explains: "*made known* . . . By what is done by the Church, which is the theatre of the divine wisdom". What a challenge to any church in any century!

Just and Faithful

The phrase occurs in Scripture at 1 John 1:9. The context and the note both refer to atonement (see chapter on 'Atonement'). This context adds further emphasis to the interpretation above of "wise and true". Wesley sees God as "just and faithful" in the matter of salvation. The meaning of justice is secondary to this, as is clear from the note at Matthew 7:2:

> [Judge not that you be not judged. For with what judgement you judge, you will be judged] Awful words! So we may, as it were, choose for ourselves whether God shall be severe or merciful to us . . . but they must expect 'judgement without mercy, who have showed no mercy'.

This understanding of God being "just and faithful" stems from the Old Testament, eg "a just God and a Saviour" (Isaiah 45:21, AV as known to Wesley). The faithfulness of God to His people is affirmed at Isaiah 45:10, 14, 17–20 and at many other places. God is faithful to His people even when they have not been faithful to Him, as in Hosea.

Wesley sees God as both faithful and just, with the meanings outlined in the note on 1 John 1:9:

> . . . *faithful* – Because He had promised this blessing, by the

unanimous voice of all His prophets. *Just* – Surely then He will punish: no; for this very reason He will pardon. This may seem strange; but upon the evangelical principle of Atonement and redemption it is undoubtedly true; because, when the debt is paid, or the purchase made, it is part of equity to cancel the bond, and consign over the purchased possession.

If we have grasped this aspect of the just and faithful God, we need have no fear about his justice at the final judgement.

Gracious and Merciful

For he maketh his sun to rise [on the evil and on the good] – He gives them such blessings, as they will receive at His hands. Spiritual blessings they will not receive. [Matthew 5:45]

God can give all His people, good and bad alike, rain and sunshine and other blessings because all are happy to receive these blessings. This note prepares the reader of the *Notes* for a stronger statement at Matthew 6:9:

Our Father – Who art good and gracious to all, our Creator, our Preserver; the Father of our Lord, of us in Him . . . the Father of the universe, of angels and men . . .

By creation and by disposition, God is good and gracious to all.

On Matthew 7:12, Wesley comments:

[Whatsoever you would that men should do to you, do you even so to them] *For this is the law and prophets* – This is the sum of all, exactly answering chapter v. 17. The whole is comprised in one word – Imitate the God of love.

In the parable of the field sown with good seed but producing weeds amongst the corn, Wesley again finds the goodness of God:

God sowed nothing but good in His whole creation . . . *An*

enemy hath done this . . . God made men, as He did angels, intelligent creatures, and consequently free either to choose good or evil; but He implanted no evil in the human soul. 'An enemy,' with man's concurrence, 'hath done this.' [Matthew 13:24, 28]

The parable of the man who gave his servants various amounts of money to use for his benefit, provides Wesley with the opportunity to make a startling observation about God at Matthew 25:24: "*I knew thou art a hard man* – No. Thou knowest Him not. He never knew God who thinks Him a hard master."

What a lovely thought about God, arising directly from the parable, as a little reflection on the man's treatment of the first and second servants shows. Verse 27 shows that the owner of the money was not asking for impossibilities from the third servant. God is not a hard master. Rather, God is so gracious that "we are permitted even to carve for ourselves! We ourselves are, as it were, to tell God how much mercy He shall show us!" (Luke 6:38).

Truly God is gracious and merciful. Further notes along this line are found at Acts 14:17; 17:26, 28; Romans 1:20; 2 Corinthians 1:3; and Hebrews 1:6.

God is love

This little sentence brought St. John more sweetness . . . than the whole world can bring. God is often styled holy, righteous, wise: but not holiness, righteousness, or wisdom in the abstract, as He is said to be love: intimating that this is His darling, His reigning attribute, the attribute that sheds an amiable glory on all His other perfections.

This note occurs at 1 John 4:8 and has implications for our understanding of all the attributes of God. Love, being His very nature, must shape our understanding, especially of atonement, and also of God's foreknowledge and omnipotence – concepts which often divide Christians. Akin to the above is his note on Hebrews 4:16: "*Unto the throne of* God, our reconciled Father, even His throne of grace – Grace erected it and reigns there".

Wesley substitutes God for the word "grace". He is correct to make this exchange because (i) God is love, and (ii) God's grace and love are identical in the experience of believers. Our approach to God in the present life should be, not with fear but with hope and joy because "Grace erected this throne and reigns there".

In his prayer recorded at John 17, Jesus addresses God as "Righteous Father" (verse 25) and prays for His disciples: "I have declared to them thy name, and will declare it: that the love wherewith thou has loved me may be in them, and I in them" (verse 26). In his note, Wesley states: "*I have declared to them thy name* – Thy new, best name of love."

On the basis that a name signifies character (as at Matthew 1:21), Wesley is correct at this point, because God is love. He is also correct because Jesus here prays for His disciples in terms of a relationship of love. The note on this verse reads –

That the love wherewith thou hast loved me [may be in them] – *and I* [may be in them] – That Thou and thy love, and I and My love, *may be in them* – That they love me with that love.

The words in brackets, which have been inserted from the Scripture text, do not appear in the note; Wesley is very economical with words!

This is the conclusion of Christ's prayer. It expresses the purpose of his coming – "to declare God's name", now seen in the words and deeds of Jesus (and about to be seen in the supreme way, in His death) as love (John 10:11,17; 15:13; Romans 5:8; Galatians 2:20; 1 John 4:8; and John 3:16). The conclusion also expresses the objective of Christ's coming – that this love, even God Himself, may be in people who will then love God with that love: "The free exercise of [God's] love . . . is the foundation of all His dispensations" (Ephesians 3:9).

Thanks be to God that He is love.

Further notes on this point are to be found at John 3:16; 20:17; Romans 1:7, 10; Hebrews 12:5,6; James 1:17, 18; 2 Peter 1:17 and cf John 1:14; and 1 John 4:19.

Notes on the power of God and the limitation of this are found at Revelation 2:21; 4:2; and 11:17.

The Trinity?
Section
8

3
Christology

WESLEY'S EXPERIENCE OF MAY 1738 centres in Christ. Through faith Wesley relates to Christ and God begins His work in him. Then Wesley actively trusts in Christ for salvation and is assured that Christ has taken away his sin and saved him.

Christology was a major issue of the eighteenth century. Thus we may expect to find Christology looming large in the *Notes*. But apart from these two 'accidents' of history, an emphasis upon Christology is inevitable in *Notes on the New Testament* from one who was a tutor in logic at the university and who laid stress on reason in his advice to believers, because the New Testament is the book of the new covenant made through Christ.

Wesley sets forth his Christology at the first opportunity, where the word Christ first occurs as a title, in the genealogy of "*Jesus, who is called Christ*" (Matthew 1:16): "The name Jesus respects chiefly the promise of blessing made to Abraham; the name Christ, the promise of the Messiah's kingdom which was made to David."

Thus at the outset Wesley identifies Jesus as the means of universal blessing promised at Genesis 12:3, and as the ruler anointed by God, promised at Isaiah 9:7 and 11:1. Then, borrowing from Heylyn, Wesley continues:

> It may be further observed, that the word Christ in Greek, and Messiah in Hebrew, signify 'Anointed'; and imply the prophetic, priestly, and royal characters which were to meet in the Messiah. Among the Jews, anointing was the ceremony whereby prophets, priests, and kings were initiated into those offices. And if we look into ourselves, we shall find a want of Christ in all these respects. We are by nature at a distance from God, alienated from Him, and incapable of a free access to Him. Hence we want a Mediator, an Intercessor; in a word, a Christ in His priestly office. This regards our state with respect to God.

And with respect to ourselves, we find a total darkness, blindness, ignorance of God, and the things of God. Now here we want Christ in His prophetic office, to enlighten our minds, and teach us the whole will of God. We find also within us a strange misrule of appetites and passions. For these we want Christ in His royal character, to reign in our hearts, and subdue all things to Himself.

Wesley's contribution to this note is indistinguishable from the words quoted from Heylyn, because it is presented in the same language and style as Heylyn used. It relates to the "prophetic" office (above) and subsequent explanation of that office in the words: "we find a total darkness, blindness . . . the whole will of God". This contribution is significant in that it shows Wesley's desire to make clear the three offices of Christ, and his readers need all three of them. This "blindness, ignorance of God" is a major element in the sermon on 'Original Sin' (*Forty-four Sermons*, No XXXVIII). Christ is utterly necessary even in this first step on the way to heaven; we need His help even to recognise our inability to find the way and "to enlighten our minds" about the things of God.

The same work of Christ appears at Matthew1:21: "*Jesus –* That is, a Saviour. It is the same name with Joshua (who was a type of Him), which properly signifies, 'the Lord, salvation.'"

Yet again at verse 23, Wesley draws attention to the nature of the work of Christ:

They shall call his name Emmanuel – To be called, only means, according to the Hebrew manner of speaking, that the person spoken of shall really and effectually be what he is called, and actually fulfil that title. Thus, 'Unto us a child is born – and his name shall be called Wonderful, Counsellor, the mighty God, the Prince of Peace'; that is, He shall be all these, though not so much nominally, as really, and in effect. And thus was He called Emmanuel, which was no common name of Christ, but points out His nature and office: as He is God incarnate, and dwells, by His Spirit, in the hearts of His people. It is observable, the words in Isaiah are, 'Thou' (namely, His Mother) 'shall call'; but here, *They* – that is, all His people, *shall call* – shall acknowledge him to be Emmanuel, God with us. *Which being interpreted* – This is a clear proof that St. Matthew wrote his Gospel in Greek, and not in Hebrew.

The phrase "only means" in the first line of this quotation might be clearer today if the words were reversed – "means only . . . that the person . . . ". It can have no other meaning than that the person . . .

For Wesley, Jesus is "the mighty God" in name (nominally), in essence (really) and in deed (in effect). It is worth noting that the Christological statement is joined with two experiential statements: "He is God incarnate, and dwells, by His Spirit, in the hearts of His people"; and "*They* . . . shall acknowledge Him to be Emmanuel, God with us", which is a fact of experience for each believer.

Twenty-seven other notes of a Christological nature on Matthew's Gospel make a strong cumulative impact – see the full list below. In this way, Wesley sets forth his ideas concerning Jesus at the very beginning of the *Notes*. To summarise, the notes on the first Gospel proclaim Jesus as the Messiah:

promised in the Old Testament: 1:16, 21, 23; 5:2; 12:23; 17:3, 5
born of a virgin: 1:25
prophet, priest and king: 1:16; 11:29; 25:14
Son of God: 2:15; 3:2, 17; 4:1, 4; 6:9; 12:49f; 17:26; 27:54
Lord (in Old Testament sense): 1:21; 3:3; 5:22
God: 1:23; 10:5; 25:9, 14; 28:18
Son of Man: 3:2; 8:20
equal to God: 5:22; 9:3
sinless: 3:16
human: 27:50;
all-knowing, all-powerful: 17:27.

True to his principle of non-repetition, Wesley has only two other notes of a Christological nature in Mark and Luke. That at

Mark 6:6 refers to the human nature of Jesus; the other, at Luke 2:49, refers to His Sonship.

Wesley has much more to say about Christology in his notes on the fourth Gospel, because he considers Saint John to have written in order to refute "those who denied His Godhead" (preface to the Gospel according to Saint Matthew). At John 1:1, Wesley comments: " . . . when at length some from hence began to doubt of His Godhead, then St. John expressly asserted it". This comment extends to 24 lines. Wesley finds the root of the term "word" firmly in the Old Testament via the Septuagint. As the Word, Jesus is "supreme, eternal, independent". But as balance to that strong final adjective, Wesley asserts that "the word rendered 'with' denotes a perpetual tendency . . . of the Son to the Father, in unity of essence".

The note at John 4:26 identifies Jesus with the Messiah, as in Matthew's Gospel. Thus Jesus, who is the fulfilment of Messianic prophecies in that Gospel, is identified with the Word of John's Gospel, the Word who is the creator of "all things" (John 1:3), and the "foundation of life to every living thing . . . fountain of wisdom, holiness, and happiness" (John 1:4). The Word "united Himself to our miserable nature, with all its innocent infirmities". The glory of God "shone forth . . . through the whole series of His life" (John 1:14).

Christological notes in the fourth Gospel proclaim Jesus as:
God, supreme, eternal, independent: 1:1, 2; 8:24, 27, 28, 58; 10:18, 30, 36; 11:41; 14:11; 20:28
one with God the father: 1:1, 18; 5:18, 19,23; 8:16, 19, 28, 29; 10:30; 14:10, 11
revealer of God: 1:1, 14,18
creator: 1:3. 4; 16:15
omnipresent: 1:10; 3:13
truly human: 1:14; 5:27
Son of God: 1:49; 5:19, 23; 8:27; 20:17
Messiah: 1:23, 26, 49; 4:26; 8:16, 19, 23 (which should be read with verses 16 and 19)

Two factors account for the differences between this list and that drawn from Matthew's Gospel. (1) Wesley is explaining the texts as they arise for the reader, and not as they might be systematically arranged by the theologian. (2) Wesley seldom repeats an explanation. Thus the term "Son of Man" is explained in the note at Matthew 3:2 according to its historical origin in Scripture, and in the note at Matthew 8:20 according to its appropriateness as applied to Jesus. Hence, no comment appears on this title at John 1:51 nor at John 3:13, while at John 5:27 Wesley interprets it to mean that Jesus "was made man", which is an addition to the meanings already given. There is no further comment on this title in John's Gospel, although it occurs at seven other places.

Christological notes found in various other books of the New Testament show Jesus to be:

God: Acts 7:59; Romans 9:5; 1 Corinthians 1:2 (to be read with note on Acts 7:59); 1 Corinthians 2:8; Ephesians 4:9; Philippians 2:6, 11; Colossians 2:9; Titus 2:13; Hebrews 1:8; 3:4; 1 John 5:20; Rev. 1:12–13, 17, 18; 19:12; 20:6, 11; 21:22; 22:16

Creator: 1 Corinthians 8:6; Colossians 1:16; Rev. 3:14

eternal: Philippians 2:6; Colossians 1:15, 17; Hebrews 1:2, 3, 4, 7; 7:3; Revelation 1:6, 14; 2:2, 18; 10:6; 19:12

one or equal with God: 1 Corinthians 8:6; Galatians 1:1; Ephesians 1:20, 21, 23; Philippians 2:6, 8, 10; Colossians 1:17, 19; 1 Thessalonians 3:11; Hebrews 1:2; Revelation 22:1, 13;

Image of God: 2 Corinthians 4:4; Colossians 1:15; Hebrews 1:1, 2, 3

Messiah: Romans 9:5; Revelation 5:9

Son of God: Acts 13:33; Galatians 4:4; Hebrews 1:3, 4–6; Revelation 2:18

human: Romans 8:3; Ephesians 1:20; Philippians 2:7, 8; Hebrews 2:17; Revelation 1:1, 12 f

sinless: Romans 8:3; 1 Peter 1:19

prophet, priest and king: Philippians 3:8; Revelation 1:1,5,12 f; 5:6, 13; 11:15; 15:4; 17:14; 19:12 f, 15; 20:11; 22:12

The notes on the verses in the three lists above make it abundantly clear that for Wesley Jesus is the Messiah/Christ of the Old Testament, that He was conceived in Mary while a virgin, and thereafter He was both truly human and truly divine; that He lived sinlessly and was the visible image of God, co-equal with the Father, eternal, creator, sustainer of all, ruling with God; that He is prophet, priest and king for all people in their relationship with God. Wesley's picture of Christ is one of traditional orthodoxy. It is the opposite of the latitudinarianism of the Church of England and the theological anarchy of some forms of Dissent in eighteenth-century England.

Wesley's other writings also bear witness to his high view of Christ. He makes his position perfectly clear in two sentences in the preface to the *Forty-four Sermons*: "God Himself has condescended to teach the way (to heaven). For this very end he came from heaven." An entry in the *Journal* (5 April 1768) reveals the importance of the Godhead of Christ to Wesley: "My subject led me to speak strongly and explicitly on the Godhead of Christ. But that I cannot help; for on this I *must* insist, as the foundation of all our hope."

Before proceeding further with this examination of the theology of the *Notes*, it seems wise to inquire into Wesley's exegesis. Are the *Notes* good exegeses of the various texts? Or did Wesley use the texts as pegs on which to hang his theological garments? On the answer to this question depends the validity of these New Testament notes as doctrinal authority, and also the validity of Wesley's claim to be a man of one book. There are notes on more than 100 verses, which relate to Christology, on 70 which relate to grace, and another 70 which relate to atonement. An enquiry into all texts relevant to Wesley's theology in the *Notes* would produce a section out of all proportion to this theological arrangement. However, a thorough examination of the 30 texts, in the notes on which Wesley describes Jesus as God, yields the following results:

1 Wesley's English text could have been translated from the United Bible Societies Greek Text (1966), except at Romans 9:5

where the difference arises from punctuation, and not from the text itself. Two hundred years of textual criticism have made no substantial changes to the Greek of these texts (Cf Kummel's first rule of exegesis). Wesley has the correct text (words) in all 30 cases.

2 At 24 of these texts, Wesley has a "correct linguistic understanding of the Greek" (Cf Kummel's second rule).

3 (a) At 20 out of the 30 texts Wesley has a correct interpretation with due regard to questions of context, authorship, readers, date, and place (Cf Kummel's third rule).

The problems relating to ten texts may be summarised thus:

(b) Matthew 28:18 and Mark 6:6: these notes seem to have been designed to rule out any interpretation which would make Jesus less than God. But exegetically they are indefensible.

(c) Wesley's translation at John 10:30 and John 14:10–11 may not be fully defensible in light of modern translations; nevertheless his notes thereon remain unaffected. For example: "*I am in the Father . . . Believe me*". This, perhaps unique, translation by Wesley makes no difference to the claim that Jesus is in the Father, nor to the note "*Because I am – God*".

(d) Romans 9:5: "[Christ] *Who is over all, God blessed for ever*".

Thus translates Wesley, Bengel, AV, and later the JB, NIV, RSV, NEB, GNB, and Greek, acknowledging this reading in footnotes. The other possible translation – " . . . is the Christ. God who is over all . . . " – appears in RSV, GNB, REB, Greek, and footnote in NIV.

Bengel devotes two pages to answering objections to the former translation. Wesley was therefore aware of the two readings and made his choice. However, if this is unacceptable, the omission of this note does not seriously affect the result of the investigation.

(e) Ephesians 4:9:

That is, does it not imply, that He descended first? Certainly it does, on the supposition of His being God. Otherwise it would not: since all the saints will ascend to heaven, though none of them descended thence.

But Wesley has forgotten that there are others in heaven, besides God, who descend, eg angels, as at John 1:51 and 5:4.

(f) Philippians 2:6: the query concerning the correct linguistic understanding of the text relates to the word harpagmos – is it active or passive in its meaning? However, the remainder of the note does not seem to be affected by this query, and so the comments concerning the deity of Christ are valid. They are supported by modern English versions, and in the commentaries of Lightfoot, Collage, and Martin.

(g) Philippians 2:11: " . . . *Lord* – Jehovah; not now 'in the form of a servant,' but enthroned *in the glory of God the Father*". Wesley follows Bengel in the translation of "eis" as "in" (Cf John 1:18). But EVV and commentaries lend no support to this; it is not a correct linguistic understanding of the text. However, the note confirms the deity of Christ by the identification of the Lord as Jehovah, which is the special name for God in the Old Testament. Hence it is acceptable and valid.

(h) Hebrews 3:4: "*Now* Christ, *he that built* not only this house, but *all things*, *is God*." Grammatically it is possible to interpret the Greek in this way, but the meaning must be decided by the context. RSV, GNB, NEB, NIV, and JB all translate so that God is the subject at this point. The note is not valid.

(i) 1 John 5:20: "*This* Jesus *is the* only living and *true God*". The note is incorrect in so far as it excludes any reference to God the Father in the demonstrative "this". It is correct in its affirmation of the Godhead of Jesus.

4. Thus at 24 out of 30 texts examined, Wesley's notes are valid and acceptable, while at Romans 9:5, where the punctuation is debatable, Wesley has good company to this today. The notes on four texts (a, b, e, h) are indefensible, while that at (i) is only half-right. In total, 24 valid notes, or 25 if Romans 9:5 is included, represents an achievement of 80 per cent or 83 per cent, a very good rate of success. From the point

of view of exegesis, although from a limited sample, the *Notes on the New Testament* reach a very respectable standard.

(Each text is investigated in my thesis – 'An Examination of John Wesley's Notes on the New Testament' – copies of which are to be found in Edgehill Theological College Library, Belfast, and the Faculty of Theology of Queen's University, Belfast. Kummel proposes these rules in his *Exegetical Method, a Student's Handbook* by Otto Kaiser and Werner G Kummel, translated by EV Groetchius, Seabury Press, New York, 1967.)

4
Sin

THE *NOTES* WERE WRITTEN FOR those who "have a desire to save their souls" (preface, paragraph 3). Such language implies danger from which people need to be saved. This danger is identified in the *Notes*, as early as the second page. Concerning the term Christ, Wesley notes:

> . . . the word [signifies] 'Anointed' . . . We are by nature at a distance from God, alienated from Him, and incapable of a free access to Him. Hence we want a Mediator . . . a Christ in His priestly office. This regards our state with respect to God. And with respect to ourselves, we find a total darkness, blindness, ignorance of God, and the things of God. Now here we want Christ in His prophetic office, to enlighten our minds, and teach us the whole will of God. We find also within us a strange misrule of appetites and passions. For these we want Christ in His royal character, to reign in our hearts, and subdue all things to Himself. [Matthew 1:16]

People are in a very perilous state, "alienated" from God, in themselves both blind toward God and unable to control their passions. Such is the nature of sin, according to Wesley; various notes confirm and expand this description.

The Nature of Sin

The idea of sin as alienation is vividly portrayed in the notes on the parable of the two sons (Luke 15:11 ff). The initial note is as explosive as a bomb, and as brief: "*Give me the part of goods that falleth to me* – See the root of all sin – a desire of disposing of ourselves, of independency on God" (verse 12). A sinner is a person who is "Far from God: God was not in all his thoughts" (verse13), one who is "without God in the world" (verse 17). Positively, this means that a sinner is a citizen "of that country which is far from God"; that is to say, he belongs to the devil (verse 15). He is truly an alien with respect to God. An extra note at the end of the parable emphasises the idea of alienation from God:

> ... sinners in their natural state ... ungratefully run from Him ... Sensual pleasures are eagerly pursued ... not a serious thought of God can find a place in their minds.

Elsewhere, the sinner is "estranged from God" (Matthew 12:39), and "sets His authority at nought" (1 John 3:4 – similar ideas appear at Matthew 6:24; 13:21; James 1:14).

Wesley acknowledges that "those things" of God, indeed, "are seen by them, and them only, who use their understanding" (Romans 1:20). Nevertheless, following Paul's description of the people of Rome, he immediately adds that "from low and base considerations [the wise heathens] conformed to the idolatry of the vulgar . . . They neither thanked [God] for His benefits, nor glorified Him for His divine perfections" (Romans 1:21). This Wesley classifies as the first degree "of ungodliness" (Romans 1:23). Reasoning, capable of knowing God in some respects, is very easily clouded over; thus reasoning leads to false knowledge, or idolatry (Romans 1:21–4). In actual experience, *"The things of the Spirit . . .* can only be discerned by the aid of that Spirit, and by those spiritual senses, which [the natural man] has not" (1 Corinthians 2:14). Without the spirit, people are ignorant of God. In the parable of the employer who gave sums of money to his employees according to the respective ability of each, when the third refers to his master/God as *"an hard man"*, Wesley enters a forthright denial: "No. Thou knowest Him not. He never knew God who thinks Him a hard master" ((Matthew 25:24). This ignorance about God has appeared above, in chapter 2: "With respect to ourselves, we find a total darkness, blindness, ignorance of God and the things of God." In the form of "base considerations", including fear (Matthew 25:25), sin distorts whatever knowledge of God the natural man can reach, and thus makes people "ignorant of God". Such is the nature of sin.

The third aspect of sin, which appears in people, is "a strange misrule of appetites and passions". This misrule, ie their power to rule even against a person's wishes, is exemplified in the notes on Romans 7:14 –25. Wesley understands these verses to relate to:

> . . . a man, reasoning, groaning, striving, and escaping from the legal to the evangelical state . . . [The natural man is] Sold under sin – Totally enslaved; slaves . . . were absolutely at their master's disposal. [verse 14]

The slave's master now takes control; the master, sin, rules even against the person's will to do good. Because the natural man, awakened to the law, does what he wishes not to do, Wesley interprets verse 17 as follows: "*It is no more I that* can properly be said to *do it, but* rather *sin that dwelleth in me.* [Sin] That makes, as it were, another person, and tyrannizes over me."

It would seem that logically Wesley should have named this person as the devil; but he chooses his words carefully and refrains from doing so in the notes on 14–15. The reason for this will become clear when the cause of sin is discussed later in this chapter.

The nature of sin is an inability to control the passions. This is a very disturbing characteristic of sin, because it is the longest lasting in ourselves, and the most damaging to other people. When people are brought near to God in Christ, and experience forgiveness, the alienating aspect of sin disappears: the ignorance of God hitherto, while not replaced by knowledge in an instant (1 Corinthians 15:34), is rendered innocuous by their "experimental religion", along with humility before God and their co-believers. But how often do old tempers, desires, fears, enmities, and prejudices remain and damage the body of Christ, and damage others also? Wesley's notes on Romans 8 show that he is aware of this problem. At the end of the struggle of

Romans 7:14–25, the "man is now utterly weary of his bondage, and upon the brink of liberty" (verse 25). "Now he comes to deliverance and liberty" (8:1). Nevertheless, Wesley writes at verse 12: "*We are not debtors to the flesh* – We ought not to follow it." If deliverance and liberty were complete, if there were an instantaneous change from one state of existence to another, Wesley ought to have written 'We do not/cannot follow it'. "Ought" implies an appeal to those who have been delivered, to take a certain course; that course they do not take automatically. The note on verse 13 tends to the same interpretation: "*If ye mortify* – Kill, destroy these [namely, evil actions, desires, tempers, thoughts]. *Ye shall live* – The life of faith more abundantly here, and hereafter the life of glory." The struggle continues. Deliverance and liberty are theoretically effected for us, but much remains to be done with regard to putting to death the old nature, where the "strange misrule of appetites and passions" is located. We are to "slay with a continued stroke" all that makes up the body of sin (Colossians 3:5; also Galatians 5:24 and 2 Peter 3:18, especially lines 5–6).

The notes on Romans 6:2, 4 and 6 also support this idea of a continuing struggle. Believers are "*Dead to sin* – Freed both from the guilt and from the power of it." But the new life does not follow mechanically from their act of faith in Christ. Wesley appeals to them that they:

> . . . *should walk in newness of life . . . Our old man . . .* our evil nature . . . in a believer is *crucified with Christ*, mortified, gradually killed, by virtue of our union with Him.

The phrase "gradually killed" is very significant; it is a window on the struggle Wesley had after 24 May 1738.[1] Also at verse 17 is an appeal, which could be unnecessary if deliverance and liberty were in practice instantaneous: " . . . our minds, all pliant and ductile, should be conformed to the gospel precepts, as liquid metals take the figure of the mould into which they are cast". But difficulty arises according to the amount of ourselves which we refuse to allow to be cast into the mould. (The notes on Matthew 6:12, 13; 13:26 and 45 imply this continuing struggle.)

Specific Sins

The notes are "explanatory". Many sins need no explanation – their meaning is very clear. Hence Wesley may pass over Scripture references to some sins without a note, while at the same place he comments on others. The well known list at Galatians 5:19–21 demonstrates this point; of the 17 sins named, Wesley comments on six – lasciviousness, idolatry, witchcraft, divisions, heresies and revellings – explaining and/or applying the meaning to the reader. The remainder – such as murder, fornication, wraths, drunkenness – need no explanation. Thus no deduction concerning the importance, or otherwise, of a sin in Wesley's estimation should be made on the basis of the presence or absence of a note. For instance, Wesley here writes, "*Revellings* – Luxurious entertainments." This is probably more an application than an explanation of the Greek word. Its importance can only be estimated by an appreciation of the wealth and poverty of that age,[2] and the standards Wesley set for the members of his societies through notes on practical Christianity.[3] One note may suffice to show the strength of his feelings on this matter: " . . . luxury punishes fraud, while it feeds disease with the fruits of injustice" (Matthew 23:25).

There are numerous notes concerning sins to which religious people are prone. An unusually long note at Matthew 23:31 applies this chapter of woes to the eighteenth-century Pharisees, in seven categories; for example, "a scrupulous exactness in little observances, though with the neglect of justice, mercy, and faith". (Also relevant are the notes at Matthew 13:28; 15:8; 25:25; Luke 15:7; and Romans 3:13.) At the other extreme within the Church are young converts who, in judging others, "are so apt to spend that zeal which is given them for better purposes!" (Matthew 7, preface; see also notes on heresies at Galatians 5:20; 2 Peter 2:1).

A major sin of religious people of that age is "negative goodness". This is Wesley's term for those who hope to be accepted by God because they "do no harm . . . honest, inoffensive, good sort of people" (Matthew 25: preface). Such people, he warns: "The same great truth that there is no such thing as negative goodness is shown in this chapter three times." In the first parable, the lamp is faith, and oil is love in one's heart. The lamp only works if it has oil in it; faith is only effective if it works by love. (Wesley often describes faith as working by love, eg James 2:14.) With regard to the second parable he asks: "Reader, art thou . . . hiding the talent God hath lent thee?" (verse 18). The privilege of being in a right relationship with God must show its appreciation thereof by positive service – "barely doing no harm" is culpable. The third parable widens this service from a particular form to all "these works of outward mercy" (verse 35 – see also James 4:17).

The list appended to this chapter displays the range of the notes on sin, eg "Not only evil actions, but evil desires, tempers, thoughts" (Romans 8:13; 6:6); "Wickedness . . . Foolishness" (Mark 7:22) are words easily understandable, but Wesley drives home their application to eighteenth-century England. (On this point see especially Matthew 6:24; 27:63; Luke 15:32; Romans 3:13 f; Ephesians 2:3; 4:26; Colossians 2:23; 3:5, 8; Hebrews 10:26; 12:1; and 1 Peter 4:2 f.)

The inter-relatedness of sins is found in the notes on Romans 1:18–32. At this point also Wesley's subservience to Scripture and his skill of exegesis combine to produce notes of a very high quality. He finds here "three degrees of ungodliness": (1) Wrong thoughts about God, verses 21–24; (2) Personal sins of a private nature, verses 25–27, the result of (1); (3) Personal sins of a public nature, verses 28–31, the result of (2). To have pleasure in those that practice such things is defined as:

> . . . the highest degree of wickedness. A man may be hurried by his passions to do the thing he hates; but he that has pleasure in those that do evil, loves wickedness for wickedness' sake. And

hereby he encourages them in sin, and heaps the guilt of others upon his own head. [verse 32]

The Cause of Sin

Wesley is in no doubt about the reality of the devil. But his understanding of the devil's activity is complex. The devil's reality is the basis of the notes on the temptations of Jesus (Matthew 4:1–11). But he notes at verse 3 that he comes: "In a visible form; probably in a human shape, as one that desired to inquire further into the evidences of His [Jesus'] being the Messiah." This is an interpretation agreeable with some current thinking of this point.[4]

Given this conviction about the reality of the devil, it would appear that Wesley should allocate to him the cause of sin. But while he comes close to this on some occasions, he never makes the identification. In the parable of the wheat and the weeds, Wesley is adamant that the weeds come "Not from the Parent of good", adding, "Even the heathen could say 'No evil from thee can proceed'" (Matthew 13:27). The next note shows the complexity of his understanding of the origin of sin:

. . . An enemy hath done this – A plain answer to the great question concerning the origin of evil. God made men, as He did angels, intelligent creatures, and consequently free either to chose good or evil; but He implanted no evil in the human soul. 'An enemy,' with man's concurrence, 'hath done this.'

The origin of evil is the devil, but he is not effective without man's agreement.[5] The note on James 1:14 emphasises both the cause and the concurrence. The former is "injections of the devil" but these "cannot hurt before we make them our own". The cause of every sin is "*in*, not *out of*, ourselves". Desire and our own will – both within – combine to produce actual sin. (James 1:15). This view of the cause of sin is also to be seen in Wesley's claim that, "Unbelief is the parent of all evil, and the very essence of unbelief lies in *departing from God*" (Hebrews

3:12 – see also Luke 15:12). Not to believe and then to depart from God are the result of our free choice.

In the note on 1 Peter 5:10, the devil's lack of power is exposed by a comparison with God's power and grace. The whole work of God is begun, continued and finished in us by His grace alone. He Himself will perfect us; we have "only to watch and resist the devil: the rest God will perform". While the devil is real and active in the problem of sin, he is not the cause of actual sin; people sin and so are guilty before God.

The Extent of Sin

"Sin and the world are of equal extent" (John 1:29); and the world is "all mankind" (John 3:3 and 6) – the same claim is made in notes at a minimum of ten other texts. Sin extends to "as many as are born into the world" (Hebrews 9:28). At 1 John 5:19, Wesley states: "*But the whole world* – All who have not His Spirit . . . *Lieth in the wicked one* – Void of life, void of sense" (see also Romans 3:23; 5:12, 16, 19; Galatians 3:22; and 1 John 1:8, 9).

Some of the notes about the extent of sin are based on the historicity of Adam. Of the climactic text "*all have sinned*" (Romans 3:23), Wesley writes: "In Adam, and in their own persons; by a sinful nature, sinful tempers, and sinful actions." The reference to Adam is justifiable as an anticipation of Romans 5:12 ff; the references to sinful natures, tempers and actions summarise the description of Romans 1:18–32. That "all have sinned" is true, not simply because all are in Adam, but because he is "the common head and representative" (Romans 5:19), a historical view of Adam as the first person which is highly questionable today. That "all have sinned" is true because "all have sinned in their own persons . . . tempers . . . actions". The note on Romans 3:23 continues: " . . . *short of the glory of God* . . . short of His image on earth". That image is the Lord Jesus; a comparison of any person with that image is sufficient to establish the truth of universal sin.

Wesley appears to present a harsh doctrine of sin with respect to infants: " . . . *death* . . . came upon *all men*, infants themselves not excepted, *in that all sinned*." (Romans 5:12). Again, at Romans 5:14, he states: "*Death reigned* . . . Even over infants who had never sinned, as Adam did, in their own persons". Two considerations may be offered in mitigation of this harshness. Firstly, Wesley is speaking of death in the physical sense; by the normal time of death, all have sinned in their own persons. At Romans 3:23 Wesley brings together the theological element "in Adam" and the existential (experimental) "in their own persons". Colin Williams speaks of "the existential account Wesley gives of the natural man".[6] It is at the existential level that people, constituted sinners on account of descent from sinners, become actual sinners and guilty. To call an infant an actual sinner is inconsistent with Wesley's dictum that God is "the Parent of good" (Matthew 13:27). Secondly, at Romans 5:19, Wesley makes a significant alteration to the AV: "*As by the disobedience of one man many* (that is all men) *were constituted* [made] *sinners*." The Greek word kathistemi is used at Matthew 25:21, 23, "I will make you ruler over many things"; here "to constitute as ruler" would be a very meaningful translation. Such constituting is of very little consequence before the ruler makes a decision. Similarly, to be "constituted sinners", which is the unavoidable consequence of Adam's sin, becomes important only when a person sins. CK Barrett lends support to this view:

> . . . the words "sinners" and "righteous" are words of relationship, not character. Adam's disobedience did not mean that all men necessarily and without their consent committed particular acts of sin; it meant that they were born into a race which had separated itself from God.[7]

And with that Wesley would have agreed: "*But the whole world* – All who have not his Spirit . . . *Lieth in the wicked one* – Void of life, void of sense" (1 John 5:19). Such is the extent of sin quantitatively.

Qualitatively sin is equally extensive: "*Our sins* . . . Spread themselves all over the whole man" (Romans 7:5). While we are without Christ, we are "*without strength* – Either to think, will, or do anything good" (Romans 5:6). The "*old man*", "our evil nature", is "Co-eval with our being"; it is as old as the person is. Our old man, Wesley feels, is "a strong and beautiful expression for that entire depravity and corruption which by nature spreads itself over the whole man, leaving no part uninfected" (Romans 6:6). Such is the extent of sin in each person. Wesley's conviction in this matter is emphasised by the notes at 2 Corinthians 5:21, Philippians 2:15, and Colossians 2:13, which include the phrases "inbred sin" and "original sin". The "corruption of human nature", Wesley asserts, "spreads through all the powers of the soul, as well as all the members of the body" (Galatians 5:21). This corruption of human nature is the basis of the note on the "blasphemy against the Spirit" (Matthew 12:31): "It is neither more nor less than the ascribing those miracles to the power of the devil which Christ wrought by the power of the Holy Ghost." (This account of the extent of sin is confirmed in the *sermon on 'Original Sin'* based on Genesis 6:58.)

The Punishment of Sin

In the beginning, "Sin is born big with death" (James 1:15). In the end, "Death is the devil's servant and sergeant, delivering to him those whom he seizes in sin" (Hebrews 2:14).

Death is the inevitable consequence of sin. The connection is made in the notes at Romans 5:12, 6:23; 1 Corinthians 15:56; Galatians 3:22; and Hebrews 9:14. Wesley interprets death in a physical sense at Romans 5:12 where the reference is made to Adam, as the means by which sin came into the world: " . . . *death* . . . *entered into the world* when it entered into being". This must refer to physical death – no other is envisaged in Genesis 3. But even here Wesley adds "With all its attendants". He does not elaborate on this phrase; however the note on 1 Corinthians 15:56 points to one of death's attendants: "Without which [sin] it [death] could have no power.".Sinners "must have been consumed by the divine justice, had not this atonement been made" (2 Corinthians 5:21). Execution of God's justice with regard to sin is one of death's attendants. Thus, "*the due wages of sin*" is death – "Temporal, spiritual, and eternal" (Romans 6:23). When sin grows up to maturity, it gives birth to death (James 1:15). This is "spiritual death in the soul, and leads to death everlasting" (Hebrews 9:14).

The nature of this death Wesley portrays in vivid language and in physical imagery at Matthew 25:41 and 46, but also with comparative brevity and even a hint of regret. The fire was prepared for the devil and his angels; Wesley adds sadly, appealing to his readers: "Not originally for you; you are intruders into everlasting fire." The reason for this brevity and sad appeal, and for the larger emphasis on the appeal for faith, love and service now may be traced to an event in Wesley's life en route to America. When some confessed faith in God during a storm, but were unchanged the next morning when the storm had passed, he wrote in the *Journal*: "But, for the future I will never believe them to obey from fear who are dead to the motives of love."[9] The Minutes of Conference, in 1745 and also 1746, both contain a warning against too great an emphasis on the wrath, and an appeal to emphasise the love of God.[10]

Wesley is surely correct in this balance. This is the age of grace; he is offering Christ to people who have a desire to save their souls. The punishment of sin, spiritual death, is real; but at this moment the love of God is all-important, and all-embracing, and his readers have an opportunity to experience this.

References
1 *Journal I**, 24 May 1738, paragraph 16 and following pages.
2 Roy Porter, *English Society in the Eighteenth Century*, Pelican.
3 See Chapter 12 below.
4 David Hill, *New Century Bible Commentary on Matthew*, pp 99 f.
5 Wesley is not really dealing with the philosophical problem of evil

but with the religious question of sin; he uses the two words interchangeably, but the context makes it clear that he is referring only to the moral evil.

6 Colin Williams, *John Wesley's Theology Today*, p 55. Cf Robert E Cushman, *John Wesley's Experimental Divinity*, pp 36 f:

> A third characteristic of "experimental divinity" is that however correct the creeds of Christendom may be on the point of "original sin", this truth is without consequence until it is owned unequivocally by the "almost" Christian . . . Both Wesley and Augustine verified in experience the truth of the originality of sin.

The note on Romans 7:9 substantiates Cushman's point.

7 CK Barrett, *Commentary on the Epistle to the Romans*, p 117. JB Phillips translates: "One man's disobedience placed all men under the threat of condemnation." How significant is the word "threat" here?

8 *Forty-four Standard Sermons*, no 38, Epworth Press, London, 1944. New Edition of *Wesley's Works*, Vol II, no 44, Abingdon Press, Nashville, Tennessee, 1985. The figures in brackets refer to divisions in this sermon.

9 *Journal I*, p 139, 18 January 1736.

10 Minutes of Conference, 1745. The business for Friday, 2 August includes:

> Q.17 Do not our assistants preach too much of the wrath and too little of the love of God?
> A. We fear that they have leaned to that extreme and hence some may have lost the joy of faith.

Minutes of Conference, 1746. The business for Wednesday, 14 May includes:

> Q.17 What inconvenience is there in speaking much of the wrath and little of the love of God?
> A. It generally hardens them that believe not and discourages

them that do.

*References to the *Journal* by Volume number are according to the Standard Edition by Nehemiah Curnock, 1938, published by Epworth Press, London.

References to Scripture Texts

Matthew: 1:16; 6:24; 7:intro; 7:1; 12:39; 13:27, 28; 14:30; 15:8,9; 23:25, 31; 25:intro. ; 25:3, 4, 18,30, 31, 41, 46; 27:63

Mark: 7:15, 22

Luke: 15:12, 13, 15, 17, 32 (extra note reviewing whole parable)

John: 1:29; 3:3, 6: 16:8, 9

Acts: 5:31

Romans 1:19, 20, 21, 23–32; 3:11–14, 23; 5:6, 12–21; 6:2, 4,6,13,17,23; 7:9, 14, 16–18, 21–25; 8:1, 13

1 Corinthians: 2:14; 15:34, 56

2 Corinthians: 5:21

Galatians: 1:4; 3:22; 5:19–21, 24

Ephesians: 2:1–3

Philippians: 2:15

Colossians: 2:13; 3:5, 8

Hebrews: 2:14; 3:12; 9:14, 28; 10:26; 12:1

James: 1:14,15; 3:9; 4:17

1 Peter: 4:2,3; 5:10

2 Peter: 2:10, 13; 3:2,3, 18

1 John: 1:7–9; 2:1–2; 3:4; 5:17, 19

5

Grace

W ESLEY'S UNDERSTANDING OF GRACE IS fundamental to his
understanding of other doctrines. His Christology which
is sound becomes warm and living when it is permeated by his
doctrine of grace, because the grace of Christ was "his own"
(John 1:17). His understanding of people, that they are
thoroughly and totally sinful, is bleak; but the grace of God is
capable of changing anyone equally thoroughly and totally. His
doctrine of atonement has been described as penal
substitutionary[1] but when this is suffused with God's "darling,
His reigning attribute" (1 John 4:8), namely love or grace, the
doctrine becomes much more intimate and personal. Wesley's
understanding of grace is bound up with his experience of
Christ, or, in his own phrase, experimental religion. This type of
religion began for Wesley on 24 May 1738:

> . . . I felt my heart strangely warmed. I felt I did trust in Christ,
> Christ alone for salvation: And an assurance was given me, that
> he had taken away *my* sins . . .

Here is the beginning of heart-religion for Wesley,
"experimental religion", religion which is a relationship with
God, a matter of direct experience. Wesley went from that
meeting and for more than 50 years he "offered Christ"[2] to
people – Christ in the same manner as he himself now knew the
Saviour, who took away his sins, and Christ also as Master
whom Wesley still served as he had served before 24 May. He
now lived under grace, but continued to serve Christ with all the
discipline which he inherited from his earlier years under the
Law.

For Wesley grace is the "free and almighty love" of God
(Galatians 1:15) and the "free love of God in Jesus Christ"
(Galatians 2:21 – the repetition of this note signifies the

importance of the concept for Wesley). Grace is the "most sincere, most free, and most abundant love" of our Lord Jesus (2 Corinthians 8:9; grace is similarly described at Romans 3:24; Ephesians 2:5, 8; and Titus 3:5). The supremacy of grace is made clear at Hebrews 4:16:

> *Let us therefore come boldly* – Without any doubt or fear. *Unto the throne of God*, our reconciled Father, even His throne of *grace* – Grace erected it, and reigns there, and dispenses all blessings in a way of mere, unmerited favour.

The note at Romans 5:21 also demonstrates the supremacy of grace in salvation. It is "the source of all our blessings". Similar notes appear at Luke 10:21; Romans 6:23; 2 Corinthians 9:8; 13:13; and Revelation 4:11. Truly grace is God's "reigning attribute" (1 John 4:8) because it is the "most sincere . . . love".

But how can people receive these blessings, who are "dead, void of life" and "utterly depraved"? This is made possible by God's prevenient grace, the grace that comes to us before the act of salvation. "*And the light shineth in the darkness*", says John, and Wesley adds, "even on fallen man. *But the darkness* – Dark, sinful man, *perceiveth it not*" (John 1:5). Nevertheless, the light shines in every man by "what is vulgarly called natural conscience, pointing out at least the general lines of good and evil" (John 1:9). In a sermon 'On Conscience,' Wesley expands this note:

> . . . properly speaking, it is not natural, but a supernatural gift of God, above all his natural endowments. No; it is not nature, but the Son of God, that is "the true light, which enlighteneth every man that cometh into the world." So that we may say to every human creature, "He," not nature, "hath showed thee, O man, what is good." And it is his Spirit which giveth thee an inward check, who causeth thee to feel uneasy, when thou walkest in any way contrary to the light which he hath given thee.[3]

Thus, *"when the Gentiles . . . do by nature the things contained in the law"*, Wesley explains "this also, strictly speaking, is by preventing grace" (Romans 2:14). On the following verse, Wesley proclaims that "the same hand which wrote the commandments on the tables of stone" wrote "the substance" in people's hearts. Grace is "the inward power of the Holy Ghost" (Acts 4:33). Thus prevenient grace is another expression for the work of the Holy Spirit as stated at John 16:8–8. He works in unbelievers to convince them of sin and thereby to present them with the choice of accepting or rejecting the righteousness which Christ offers. By His grace "alone we can come to the Father" (2 Corinthians 13:13). At John 6:44, Wesley asserts: "No man can believe in Christ, unless God give him power." (This message is repeated at Acts 13:48.) Thus "the riches of God's grace . . . reserves to Him the entire glory of our salvation, and hides pride from man" (Luke 10:21).

Wesley's conviction about the universality of grace is expressed in many notes:

God so loved the world – That is, all men under heaven; even those that despise His love, and will for that cause finally perish. [John 3:16]

. . . God is not a respecter of persons – Is not partial in His love. The words mean . . . in a general [sense], that He is loving to every man, and willeth all men should be saved. [Acts 10:34]

Christ . . . Jesus . . . Came into the world to save sinners – All sinners, without exception. [1 Timothy 1:15]

Out of his own experience he writes:

It is strange that any whom He has actually saved should doubt the universality of His grace! [1 Timothy 2:3]

The long note at the conclusion of the parable of the two sons is only meaningful on the assumption that all who "see themselves naked, indigent, and undone" may return to the Father (Luke 15:32; similar notes appear at John 17:2 and 1 Corinthians 8:11). Nothing less than "to redeem mankind" Wesley sees as the objective of "the determinate counsel of His love" (Acts 2:23).

Although grace is universally available, some "despise God's love and will for that cause finally perish"; some will be "finally impenitent" (Romans 8:19). Although grace is "almighty love" (Galatians 1:15), love is "God's reigning attribute" and so His omnipotence cannot coerce people to enter into a saving relationship. Wesley makes this point directly at Acts 2:23. At the crucifixion God did not "blast all their designs . . . because He 'so loved the world'; because it was the determinate counsel of His love, to redeem mankind from eternal death". Grace is not irresistible. God "draws us first by good desires, not by compulsion, not by laying the will under any necessity; but by the strong and sweet, yet still resistible, motions of his heavenly grace" (John 6:44; similar notes are at Acts 13:48; 26:19). As for the blessings of salvation, the "almighty Lord . . . invites us, entreats us, and, with the most tender importunity, solicits us, not to reject them" (2 Corinthians 5:20).

Further, grace can be rejected even after it has been accepted, according to Wesley – it is always resistible. The note on 1 Corinthians 9:27 is a clear warning to those who consider themselves saved:

This single text may give us a just notion of the scriptural doctrine of election and reprobation; and clearly shows us, that particular persons are not in Holy Writ represented as elected absolutely and unconditionally to eternal life, or predestinated absolutely and unconditionally to eternal death; but that believers in general are elected to enjoy the Christian privileges on earth; which if they abuse, those very elect persons will become reprobate. St. Paul was certainly an elect person, if ever there was one; and yet he declares it was possible he himself might *become a reprobate*. Nay, he actually would have become such, if he had not thus kept his body under, even though he had been so long an elect person, a Christian, and an apostle.

Wesley notes that "even this grace whereby St. Paul was influenced was not irresistible" (Acts 26:19). With incisive logic he comments concerning the parable of the two debtors:

(1) The debtor was freely and fully forgiven; (2) he wilfully and grievously offended; (3) his pardon was retracted . . . And shall we still say, But when we are once freely and fully forgiven, our pardon can never be retracted? [Matthew 18:34]

Wesley makes a similar deduction at John 15:9. (See also John 5:24 and 6:39.) Concerning those who "*make shipwreck of their faith*", Wesley's note could scarcely be stronger:

Indeed, none can make shipwreck of faith who never had it. These, therefore, were once true believers: yet they fell not only foully, but finally; for ships once wrecked cannot be afterwards saved. [1 Timothy 1:19]

Wesley has no doubt that grace is resistible both before and after acceptance of salvation.

Among the sources of the *Notes on the New Testament*, are two predestinarians – Doddridge and Guyse. Although Wesley is refuting their views at this point, he uses some of their comments. An example, taken from Doddridge, is found at Romans 9:13, where Wesley quotes verbatim: " . . . this does not relate to the person of Jacob or Esau; (2) nor does it relate to the eternal state either of them or their posterity". It is significant that the notes on Romans 9 contain much more material from Wesley than is usual, and some from an unnamed source. (His dependence on Bengel, Guyse and Doddridge is 29.5 per cent (64 lines out of 217; in 30 chapters analysed the average is 40 per cent[4]). Wesley is stating his case for himself, making use of whatever he considers helpful, but it is his own case.

A comparison of Matthew Henry's treatment of Romans 8:29–30 with that of Wesley illustrates the depth of the latter's exegesis. First, Henry:

> All that God designed for glory and happiness as the end, he decreed to grace and holiness as the way . . . All that God did from eternity predestinate to grace and glory, he does, in the fullness of time, effectually call . . . All that are effectually called are justified, absolved from guilt, and accepted as righteous, through Jesus Christ . . . The power of corruption being broken in effectual calling and the guilt of sin removed in justification, all that hinders is taken out of the way and nothing can come between that soul and glory.

(The concluding statement is equivalent to final perseverance.) Henry is so anxious to extol the sovereignty of God that he gives the impression of a mechanical activity of God, proceeding, whatever man does, to its conclusion.

Wesley's notes on these verses should be read at this point, carefully. He makes four significant points:

(1) Verse 29 is joined to verse 28 by the conjunction "for". The latter speaks of the "purpose" of God. This is a "new proposition". Verses 29–30 contain the steps which God takes to achieve that purpose. Verses 17–28 and 31–39 are Paul's account of the suffering which comes to Christians due to opposition and persecution. Such suffering comes to those who "*are called according to his purpose*" (verse 28). This purpose is itemised in verses 29 and 30: " . . . this is the method whereby God leads us step by step toward heaven".

(2) What we call the decrees of God are "only a popular representation of His infallible knowledge and unchangeable wisdom". There is no need of such decrees in respect of "Him who sees all things at one view". Wesley ridicules the idea that before creation God had to make decrees about who should go

to heaven and who should not. This is merely a human way of thinking due to the effect of God's method.

(3) How do we know who are predestinated? They have the mark of "*being conformable to the image of his Son*". This is "the general use [coming] from the whole [doctrine]" (Romans 12:1). The practical, the observable, is more important than the speculative.

(4) Nowhere does Saint Paul affirm that "precisely the same number of men are called, justified, and glorified". Paul was writing to those who are "*beloved of God, called and holy*" (Romans 1:7). They could reasonably consider themselves to be on the third step; but Wesley notes that Paul himself inserts a warning: "Provided they 'continued in His goodness' (Rom. xi 22), *he* in the end *glorified*" (Romans 8:30).

Wesley interprets Scripture by Scripture, and also by reason but without exalting the latter thereby. His use of both tools tends rather to the glory of God, the creator of reason, than to man, the user of it. Thus Wesley shows how a text apparently favourable to the predestination position may be interpreted without giving support to this.

Some parts of Romans 9 also appear to support this view, but for Wesley this is a fundamental error of exegesis. He prefaces the notes on this chapter with a survey of the whole. This preface to Romans 9 should be read, and also Romans 8:33. He argues:

> . . . St. Paul . . . had not here the least thought of personal election or reprobation . . . (1) because it lay quite wide of his design . . . (2) because such a doctrine . . . would have evidently tended to harden the Jews . . . (3) because when he sums up his argument . . . he has not one word . . . about it.

Wesley has anticipated the modern rule of exegesis, namely, "of setting the statements of the individual passages in their context in the writing or the corpus of writings concerned".[5] For example, Wesley notes that the prophecy, "*The elder shall serve the younger"* (Romans 9:12) could not have been applied to the individuals named because Esau in person did not serve Jacob, but he did "in his posterity". Again, and correctly, Wesley notes that the quotation in the next verse was true when Malachi wrote the words, true of the nations descended from the twins, but not of the twins themselves. Truly there is "not here the least thought of election or reprobation".

The principle, enunciated to Moses, "*I will have mercy on whom I will have mercy"* Romans (9:15), is based on the sovereignty of God who fixes the terms on which people receive compassion: " . . . who accept of it in this way that I have appointed" (Romans 9:15 and also 17). This is the way of belief (Romans 9:18). The notes on the following verses are directed to the charge of injustice in God. Matthew Henry avoids this charge:

> [1] by reproving the objector . . . this is not an objection fit to be made by the creature against his Creator . . . [2] by resolving all into the divine sovereignty . . . The rude and unformed mass of matter hath no right to this or that form but is shaped at the pleasure of him that formed it.

This is a very unsatisfying position because (1) in as much as the objector is a creature made in the image of God, it is a fit question; (2) Henry equates "the rude and unformed mass of matter" with the creature formed by God; it is the latter not the former that has some rights in this problem; and (3) Henry assumes that the "rude and unformed mass of matter" is claiming a right to this or that shape; the text of Scripture merely asks the question 'Why have I this shape?' Wesley cannot rest in such a position as Henry's, because God's will "is not the will of an arbitrary, capricious, or tyrannical being. He wills nothing but what is infinitely wise and good" (Romans 9:21). Hence the question, "*Why hast thou made me thus?*" is interpreted by Wesley to mean, "Why hast Thou made me capable of honour and immortality, only by believing?"

(Romans 9:20). God has the right to "appoint *one vessel*, namely, the believer, *to honour*, *and another*, the unbeliever, t*o dishonour?*".

This interpretation is in harmony with the main purpose of Romans 9:11, namely, to explain what has happened to the Jews, God's chosen people. They are His people still if they believe, as was the case throughout their history. All who believe, Jews and Gentiles, are vessels of mercy (Romans 9:23–24).

In an extra note following that on 9:21, Wesley distinguishes between God "as Creator, Proprietor, and Lord of all" and God as "moral Governor, and Judge" of His intelligent creatures (a distinction which also appears at Mark 3:13). As regards the former, there are aspects of our lives which we may not understand, eg the time and place of our existence, and, as he writes:

> . . . our constitution of body and turn of mind . . . But God's methods of dealing with us, as our Governor and Judge, are . . . revealed . . . He will finally reward every man according to his works: 'He that believeth shall be saved, and he that believeth not shall be damned.'

Thus Wesley allows no space to predestination of individuals. Those who are "fitted for destruction" become so "by their own wilful and final impenitence". He is concerned to refute the charge that there is injustice in God. God has always dealt with people on the basis of faith. Hence the Gentiles have now come into a right relationship with God (Romans 9:30) and Jews have not:

> And *wherefore* have they not? Is it because God eternally decreed they should not? There is nothing like this to be met with; but agreeable to his argument the apostle gives us this good reason for it, *Because they sought it not by faith* – Whereby alone it could be attained . . . *For they stumbled at that*

stumblingstone – Christ crucified. [Romans 9:32]

Thus Wesley keeps the prime purpose of the *Notes* to the fore, to "write chiefly for plain, unlettered men, who . . . reverence and love the Word of God, and have a desire to save their souls".[6]

At Romans 9:18, Wesley interprets "*He hardeneth*" to mean "Leaves to the hardness of their hearts", and later, "suffers to be hardened in consequence of their obstinate wickedness" (extra note following that on Romans 9:21). This is in agreement with the repeated phrase of Romans 1, "God gave them up."[7] Sanday and Headlam also connect the two phrases.[8] While they note that such passages "must be balanced by others which imply the Divine love and human freedom", they maintain that there is no necessity to soften the words at Romans 9:18 on the grounds that Paul is arguing against a typical Jewish opponent who is bound to accept the words in their Old Testament context. However true that may be for Paul in the first century vis-à-vis a typical Jew, to accept them in this hard sense is difficult for Christians of later centuries, who read the Old Testament in the light of the New. Wesley softens the words. For this he has prepared the way in the notes on Mark 6:52 and 8:17–18. Hardened in the former context means to be "slow and dull of apprehension". In the latter, referring to the apostles, Wesley notes:

. . . it is certain that they were not judicially hardened. Therefore all these strong expressions do not necessarily import anything more than the present want of spiritual understanding.

Judicially hardened means "hardened by God as a punishment for sin".[9]

In the notes on the Old Testament, ten years later, Wesley interprets:

Now the Lord hardened Pharaoh's heart – Before he had

hardened his own heart, and resisted the grace of God, and now God justly gave him up to his own heart's lusts, to strong delusions, permitting Satan to blind and harden him. Wilful hardness is commonly punished with judicial hardness. Let us dread this as the sorest judgement a man can be under on this side of hell. [Exodus 9:12. Acts 28:26 contains a similar thought.]

Once again Wesley interprets Scripture by Scripture, when he notes that previously Pharaoh had hardened his own heart, for example at Exodus 8:15, 32. At the conclusion of the plagues prior to Exodus 9:12, the phrase is "Pharaoh hardened", or "his heart was hardened", no agent being specified. Wesley is surely correct in his interpretation of 9:12. The idea of an opportunity given to Pharaoh to comply with the demand of God to let his people go, reappears in the note at Romans 9:17. The plagues were designed to show God's power over "the natural causes of their health, diseases, life, and death", and also over the idols worshipped by the Egyptians, "in order . . . to draw them . . . to worship the one God". Thus Pharaoh is:

> . . . a man, not whom He made wicked on purpose, but whom He found so . . . and who, being incorrigible, well deserved to be set up in that situation, where the divine judgements fell the heaviest.

oh dear!

Wesley allows no space to predestination in the sense of an eternal decree that made Pharaoh harden his heart. "One of Mr. Wesley's preachers", CK Barrett, considers predestination to be:

> . . . the most comfortable of all Christian doctrines if man will accept it in its Biblical form and not attempt to pry into it with questions which it does not set out to answer. It is not a "quantitative limitation of God's action but a qualitative definition", the final statement of the truth that justification, and in the end salvation also, are by grace alone.

The quotation within the quotation is from Barth's commentary on Romans. If this is the meaning of predestination, then truly Methodists have "come to the very edge of Calvinism", as the 1745 Conference declared!

Predestination, understood as a definition of the purpose of God, appears again in the notes on Ephesians 1:5 and 11; these are the only other texts in which the word occurs in the New Testament (AV). It means simply that God "foreordained that all who afterwards believed should enjoy the dignity of being sons of God, and joint-heirs with Christ". Wesley continues, using a parody of the common form of predestination:

> The unalterable decree [which is made after the counsel of His own will is] 'He that believeth shall be delivered'; which *will* is not an arbitrary will, but flowing from the rectitude of His nature: else, what security would there be that it would be His *will* to keep His word even with the elect?

We know God's nature – holiness, justice, love, power: taking all these together and adding the doctrine of atonement, the predestination of believers is "the most comfortable of all Christian doctrines". The note on John 3:16 reduces the doctrine of double predestination as an absurdity. (Further notes on predestination appear at Matthew 20:15 f; John 6:40, 64; 12:39; Acts 9:15; 1 Timothy 1:13; Hebrews 6:11; and Jude 6.)

The doctrine of final perseverance (Westminster Confession, chapter 17) receives many sharp shocks from Wesley. The possibility of falling away was there, even for Paul, "an elect person, if ever there was one", exclaims Wesley at 1 Corinthians 9:27. This may be regarded as only hypothetical; however, Judas provides a factual example, as Wesley contends in the notes on John 6:70 and 17:12. Unqualified promises made to the disciples by our Lord must have a condition implied. This is obviously the case at Matthew 19:28:

> *Ye shall sit . . . On twelve thrones* – So our Lord promised,

without expressing any condition: yet, as absolute as the words are, it is certain there is a condition implied . . . these twelve did not sit on those twelve thrones; for the throne of Judas another took, so that he never sat thereon.

Likewise, to the promise of Christ, "*And cometh not into condemnation*", Wesley adds the condition, "Unless he make shipwreck of the faith" (John 5:24). Believers must "endure to the end" (John 6:37, 39). The "elect", whom God's angels will gather together, are "all that have endured to the end in 'the faith that worketh by love'" (Matthew 24:31). The doctrine of final perseverance implies for Wesley continued belief and obedience. Both the doctrine and the implicit condition Wesley expresses beautifully at John 14:19:

Because I live, ye shall live also – Because I am the Living One in My divine nature, and shall rise again in My human nature, and live for ever in heaven; therefore, ye shall live the life of faith and love on earth, and hereafter the life of glory.

Amen. Thanks be to God.

References

1 Colin Williams, *John Wesley's Theology Today*, p 83 ff.

2 The phrase occurs in the Minutes of the First Conference, 1744, as part of the answer to the question: "What is the best general method in preaching?" It also occurs in the Journals of both John and Charles Wesley.

3 *Works* Vol VII, Zondervan Publishing House, pp 186–94. Text – 2 Corinthians 1:12. Also New edition of *Works* by Oxford/Abingdon, Vol 3, Sermon 105. With regard to prevenient grace, see Colin Williams, *John Wesley's Theology Today*, pp 41–6.

4 Analysis in MTh thesis 'Examination of John Wesley's Notes on the New Testament,' in the Library of Edgehill Theological College, Belfast; also in the Faculty of Theology, Queen's University, Belfast.

5 See final three lines of Chapter 3 – 'Christology.'

6 Preface to the *Notes*, paragraph 3.

7 The interpretation of Scripture by Scripture is one of Wesley's principles of exegesis, and so it is possible that he had in mind here the words of Romans 1.

8 Sanday and Headlam: Commentary on Romans in ICC. The note occurs at 9:17: "The Divine Sovereignty in the Old Testament."

9 John Lawson, *Selections from John Wesley's Notes on the New Testament*, p 111.

10 CK Barrett, *A Commentary on the Epistle to the Romans*, p 171 following 8:30.

References to Scripture Texts

Matthew: 18:34; 20:15–16; 24:31; 25:13

Mark: 6:52; 8:17–18

Luke: 10:21; 15:32, (after the note on this verse, Wesley adds a review of the whole parable); 21:18

John: 1:5, 9; 3:16; 5:24; 6:37, 39–40, 44, 64, 70; 12:39; 14:19; 15:9; 17:2, 12

Acts: 2:23; 9:15; 10:34; 13:48; 17:30; 26:19

Romans: 2:14; 3:24; 5:21; 6:23; 8:19; 11:22; 8:28–30; Chapters 9–11 (In these two places Wesley offers a continuous refutation of predestination.)

1 Corinthians: 8:11; 9:27

2 Corinthians: 5:20; 8:9; 9:8; 13:13

Galatians: 1:15; 2:21

Ephesians: 1:5, 11; 2:5, 8

Philippians: 2:13

Colossians: 2:14

1 Timothy: 1:13, 15, 19; 2:3

Titus: 3:5

Hebrews: 1:14; 2:9; 4:16; 10:29

2 Peter: 1:10

Revelation: 2:21

6
Atonement

THE CROSS IS THE SYMBOL of Christianity; the interpretation of the cross is the theological centre of Christianity. The symbol has many forms; and so has the interpretation. Sometimes these have become the main bond between Christians, and sometimes the main division. Thus, great care should be taken to understand Wesley at this point, especially as he proclaimed himself, and his followers, "to be friends of all".

Christological notes are abundant in Matthew, John, Acts and the Epistles (see Chapter 3, 'Christology'). Wesley is certain that Jesus is God. This is the basis on which the interpretation of the atonement must stand. The light which should guide this interpretation is found in the note at 1 John 4:8:

> *God is love* – This little sentence brought St. John more sweetness, even in the time he was writing it, than the whole world can bring. God is often styled holy, righteous, wise; but not holiness, righteousness or wisdom in the abstract, as He is said to be love: intimating that this is His darling, His reigning attribute, the attribute that sheds an amiable glory on all His other perfections.[1]

The note on Hebrews 4:16 makes the same point: " . . . *the throne of God* . . . Grace erected it, and reigns there". Wesley's interpretation of the atonement at specific texts must be understood in the light of the love of God. Further, Wesley believes that he has provided an interpretation in which "all the attributes [of God] harmonize; every attribute is glorified, and not one superseded, no, nor so much as clouded" (Romans 3:26). These three affirmations – that Jesus is God, that love is supreme, and that God is harmonious within himself – are fundamental to Wesley's interpretation of the atonement.

The Necessity for Atonement

This is two-fold. The first reason arises from the sinful nature of people, as demonstrated in Chapter 4. They are "alienated from" God and in "total darkness, blindness, ignorance of God" (Matthew 1:16); they are "sold under sin – totally enslaved". The whole person is infected with "entire depravity and corruption" (Romans 6:6); "inwardly and outwardly nothing but sin" (2 Corinthians 5:21). The *"whole world . . . Lieth in the wicked one* – Void of life, void of sense" (1 John 5:19). The whole world and the whole person need atonement. The second reason for atonement arises from the nature of God – His righteousness is "eternal, essential" and "includes both justice and mercy" (Romans 1:17). It also includes "vindictive justice whose essential character and principal office is, to punish sin" (Romans 3:25). God must "evidence Himself to be strictly and inviolably righteous in the administration of His government . . . The attribute of justice must be preserved inviolate" (Romans 3:26). Hence there must be atonement for sin. Other notes which relate the atonement to the justice of God are at Matthew 26: 37; 27:45 f; Mark 15:34; 2 Corinthians 5:21; Philippians 2:7; Hebrews 5:7; 9:26, 28; 1 Peter 2:24; 2 Peter 1:1; and 1 John 1:9 – a substantial number. "One punishment of sin is from the very nature of it . . . another . . . is from vindictive justice" (Romans 1:24). Wesley seems to be using the word 'vindictive' in the sense of retributive.[2]

Similar to the concept of the justice of God is that of his wrath. A very clear example of this similarity occurs at Revelation 19:15: *"And he treadeth the winepress of the wrath of God* – That is, He executes His judgements on the ungodly." The wrath of God is his justice executed upon people. Out of 27 references to the wrath of God in the New Testament, Wesley comments on half of them. This is a high proportion in the face of the brevity of the notes. Wesley seldom repeats a note. The notes on Mark 10–15 are very few compared to those on Matthew 19–27. In Matthew's Gospel he has provided almost all the notes which he considers necessary. See also at

1 John: 2:2.

Wesley is careful to guard against misunderstanding the concept of the wrath of God. Both love and wrath are human passions. But "wrath in God is not a human passion; nor is love, as it is in God" (Romans 5:9). Just as love in God is defined by His actions in relation to the world, so is the wrath of God. It is the justice of God as experienced by people; it is intimately linked to law and justice (Romans 1:17 and Revelation 19:15), and is untainted by injustice (Romans 9:22). In the note at 1 John 2:2, Wesley describes propitiation as the "atoning sacrifice, by which the wrath of God is appeased". This note, when taken by itself, might allow the wrath of God to be understood as an outburst of anger. Perhaps Wesley should not have used the word "appeased". But he is sure that God can be "offended" (Romans 3:25) by sin and angry at it. Hence "appeased" may be accepted as appropriate and meaningful in this context.

It is worth noting that Wesley, long before the publication of the *Notes*, had laid down guidelines for his preachers concerning this aspect of the Gospel. In the Minutes of Conference for 1745 there appears the following:

> Q. Do not our assistants preach too much of the wrath and too little of the love of God?
> A. We fear they have leaned to that extreme and hence some may have lost the joy of faith.

1? 47

The conference of 1746 went further, declaring that "speaking much of the wrath and little of the love of God generally hardens them that believe not and discourages them that do."[3] Nevertheless, where the concept appears in Scripture, Wesley does not avoid it; he "assists" those "who have a desire to save their souls" to understand it. (Other notes on the wrath of God occur at Matthew 27:46; Luke 22:44; Romans 2:8; Colossians 1:14; and Revelation 14:10; 15:1).

The Initiative towards the Atonement

The above interpretation of wrath is confirmed when the atonement is seen as the work of God, Father, Son and Holy Spirit, and not of one member of the Trinity against another. Making this point at Hebrews 9:14, Wesley claims that the work of redemption is the work of the whole Trinity:

> Neither is the Second Person alone concerned even in the amazing condescension that was needful to complete it. The Father delivers up the kingdom to the Son; and the Holy Ghost becomes the gift of the Messiah, being, as it were, sent according to His good pleasure.

Again, "The whole Godhead, but more eminently, God the Father" was in Christ reconciling the world to Himself (2 Corinthians 5:19). The fullness of the time for the coming of the Saviour into the world was "Appointed by the Father" (Galatians 4:4). Further, God sent His Son "From His own bosom". Wesley has already interpreted this phrase to mean "the highest unity, and most intimate knowledge" (John 1:18). The initiative towards atonement is that of God, Father and Son. The work of atonement is done by God, Father, Son and Holy Spirit (Titus 3:5).

That Wesley sees the atonement in the light of the love of God is clearly seen at 1 John 4:8 and Hebrews 4:16. The very design of God's love was to give people "spiritual health" by sending His Son into the world (John 3:15 f). Wesley translates Romans 5:8:

> *But God recommendeth* [his love towards us] – A most elegant expression. Those are wont to be recommended to us, who were before either unknown to, or alienated from, us.

The words "unknown" and "alienated" echo the description of the human state described at Matthew 1:16 – our need of Christ in His three-fold office.

The initiative is certainly God's, sometimes referring to God the Father alone. The work of atonement is that of Father, Son and Holy Spirit.

At Hebrews 10, Wesley draws attention to the fact that the will of God was "done and suffered by Christ" (verse 10). The words of the Psalm quoted here are the words of Jesus, "*I come to do thy will*", and Wesley explains, "By the sacrifice of myself" (verse 7) and "To offer a more acceptable sacrifice; and by this very act *he taketh away the* legal, *that he may establish the* evangelical, dispensation" (verse 9). Christ is active in this scheme of salvation; he does the will of God – "The gracious scheme of salvation by faith, which depends on His own sovereign will alone" (Ephesians 1:9). The notes on Ephesians 1:8–11, and also Hebrews 5:7, are making or assuming this same point.

Perhaps the most startling note about the atonement being the work of God without distinction between Father and Son occurs at John 8:28. Wesley takes "the liberty . . . to make here . . . a small alteration" (preface, paragraph 4): "*When ye shall have lifted up the Son of man, then shall ye know that I AM, and that I do nothing of myself.*" The note thereon reads: "*That I AM* – God overall. *And that I do nothing of myself* – Being one with the Father." The unity of Jesus with God the Father, preceded by the words "*lifted up* – On the cross", must be borne in mind in any attempt to understand Wesley's interpretation of the atonement. The quotation in the note on Matthew 27:45 makes the same point: "Either the God of nature suffers, or the frame of the world is dissolved." Because Jesus is human and is also God, the God of nature suffers. His only escape would be to dissolve the laws of nature by freeing Himself from his body.

The Act of Atonement

The initiative towards the atonement comes directly from God; the act of atonement is made by Jesus, Son of God, and this is His purpose in coming into the world: "*I come to do thy will* – By the sacrifice of Myself" (Hebrews 10:7). Jesus came to do, not merely to suffer, God's will. Wesley makes this very clear at the beginning of our Lord's public ministry. He undergoes baptism at the hands of John that he "may fully perform, every part of the righteous law of God, and the commission He hath given Me" (Matthew 3:15). This active obedience extends to the moment of death. The note on Matthew 27:50, "*He dismissed his spirit*" – Wesley's own translation in lieu of "he yielded up the ghost" (AV) – is probably unique and perhaps naïve, but it affirms strongly the active obedience of Jesus even in his death:

> He died by a voluntary act of His own, in a way peculiar to Himself . . . He did not use His power to quit His body as soon as it was fastened to the cross . . . but continued His abode in it, with a steady resolution, as long as it was proper.

The notes on John 10:17f are to the same effect: "*I lay down my life* . . . I cheerfully die to expiate the sins of men . . . *I lay it down of myself* – By My own free act and deed." (See also John 12:27; Romans 5:19; Philippians 2:8 f; Colossians 1:14; and Hebrews 5:7 f.)

Wesley's affirmation of the humanity of Jesus has been examined under the heading of Christology; John 1:14 is worth reading again. Some of these affirmations occur in notes on the crucifixion, eg at Philippians 2:7 f – Jesus appeared "in the likeness of the fallen creatures" (see also Colossians 1:22). Thus the sufferings of Jesus were very real. He refused the drink offered to him on the cross "determining to bear the full force of His pains" (Matthew 27:34). In a very sensitive note on Mark 10:38, Wesley regards the drinking of the cup as the "inward" sufferings of Christ, and the baptism as the "outward", and adds, "Our lord was filled with sufferings within, and covered with them without."

The atonement, while being the act of the man Jesus, is equally the act of the Son of God. No human person has the power to "continue in the body as long as it is proper". Wesley sees Jesus "dying . . . like the Prince of Life" (Matthew 27:50). That it is the Son of God who died on the cross is made clear in notes at Acts 20:28; 2 Corinthians 5:19; and Hebrews 2:10; 4:14. As the humanity of Jesus is fully affirmed in relation to the cross, likewise is the divinity. At Philippians 2, Wesley explains the nature of the pre-existent Son (verse 6), the incarnate Son (verse 7), and the suffering Son. Jesus has:

> The incommunicable nature. *Of God* – From eternity . . . real God . . . real and proper *equality* . . . the fullness [sic] and the supreme height of the Godhead . . . He was content . . . to be made in the likeness of the fallen creatures . . . A real man, like other men . . . A common man . . . *Becoming obedient* – To God, though equal with Him. *Even unto death* – The greatest instance both of humiliation and obedience. *Yea, the death of the cross* – Inflicted on few but servants or slaves. [Philippians 2:6–8]

The sufferings of Jesus in body and in spirit are real. Wesley understands the cry of dereliction to express God's:

> . . . letting loose the powers of darkness upon Him, withdrawing the comfortable discoveries of His presence, and filling His soul with a terrible sense of the wrath due to the sins which He was bearing. [Matthew 27:46]

The act of atonement was made by Jesus, fully divine, truly human and really suffering.

The Result of Atonement

The *Notes* are unequivocal on this point. At Romans 3:23–4, Wesley describes people as sinful in their nature, tempers and actions; they fall short of God's "image on earth" and they cannot expect "the enjoyment of Him in heaven". Nevertheless, they "*are justified* – Pardoned and accepted". The same words occur at Romans 3:20; 4:7; 5:19; 8:30; 1 Corinthians 6:11; Colossians 1:14; Titus 3:5; Hebrews 8:12; and 1 John 1:9.

Commenting on 1 John, Wesley breaks into the sequence of the words of Scripture:

> . . . *he is faithful* [and] *Just* – Surely then he will punish: no; for this reason He will pardon. This may seem strange; but upon the evangelical principle of atonement and redemption it is undoubtedly true; because, when the debt is paid, or the purchase made, it is the part of equity to cancel the bond, and consign over the purchased possession. [1 John 1:9]

Forgiveness blots out sin and removes punishment. But this by itself could be cold and legal; it does not necessarily establish a relationship between forgiver and forgiven. The second word in Wesley's interpretation of 'justified' is equally important, "pardoned and accepted" (also at John 1:14 and 2 Corinthians 8:12). Further notes go far beyond forgiveness:

> . . . the sin is remitted, and pardon is applied to the soul . . . by the Holy Ghost, who then begins the great work of inward sanctification. [Romans 4:5]

> . . . *forgiveness* is the beginning of redemption, as the resurrection is the completion of it. [Colossians 1:14]

So extensive is the atonement. But more immediately, Christ has "*slain* – By His own death on the cross. *The enmity* – Which had been between sinners and God" (Ephesians 2:16). Wesley analyses the nature and origin of this enmity in the notes on Colossians 1:21–2, attending to each phrase of Scripture:

> *And you that were alienated, and enemies* – Actual alienation of affection makes habitual enmity. *In your mind* – Both your understanding and your affections. *By wicked works* – Which continually feed and increase inward alienation from, and enmity to, God. *He hath now reconciled* – From the moment ye believed . . . *Through death* – Whereby He purchased the reconciliation which we receive by faith. *To present you* – The

very end of that reconciliation. *Holy* – Toward God. *Spotless* –
In yourselves. *Unreprovable* – As to your neighbour.

This is "the glorious hope of perfect love" (Colossians 1:23),
and "inward sanctification" (Romans 4:5). Atonement results in
not only reconciliation, but also new nature springing from that
reconciliation. The self-offering of Christ opens the way for
believers to "*serve the living god* – In the life of faith, in perfect
love and spotless holiness" (Hebrews 9:14).

The atonement is for all. Wesley's training in logic at Oxford,
comes to the fore in the note on John 3:16. He is not content to
equate the world with all people: he demonstrates that an
interpretation less than this is illogical (see the *Notes*). At Mark
10:45, Wesley notes that Christ gave his life "*A ransom for
many* – Even for as many souls as needed such a ransom (2
Corinthians 5:15)." (There is a similar note at Hebrews 9:28.)
Wesley interprets Scripture by Scripture. The Corinthian text
says, "*he died for all*" and so the Markan "many" must mean
that the ransom was for all, but is effective only for the many
who believe in Jesus (similarly Romans 5:19). The notes on 1
Timothy 2:4–6 emphasise the universal value of the atonement;
indeed "this ransom, from the dignity of the person redeeming,
was more than equivalent to all mankind". While the Calvinists
speak of God's "eternal decrees", Wesley writes of "His
gracious *decrees*, that Christ should come into the world to save
sinners, and that whosoever believeth on Him should have
everlasting life" (Colossians 2:14). Again, " . . . *his decrees* . . .
offer mercy to all" (Ephesians 2:15).[4] Long notes at Romans
8:28 and 33, and throughout Romans 9 provide a non-Calvinist
interpretation of election. The climax comes at 9:30–2:

> . . . *Israel* – The Jews . . . *Have not attained to the law of
> righteousness* . . . And *wherefore* have they not? Is it because
> God eternally decreed they should not? There is nothing like this
> to be met with; but agreeable to his argument the apostle gives
> us this good reason for it, *Because they sought it not by faith* –

Whereby alone it could be attained.

As Wesley comments at Ephesians 1:11, "The unalterable decree, 'He that believeth shall be delivered' . . . ". The only limitation on atonement is unbelief.

So far, attention has been focussed on the result of the atonement on people. Has the atonement an effect on or in God? In as much as the atonement was necessary on account of the wrath of God, it has an effect on God. At Romans 3:25, Wesley makes no attempt to alter or soften the word "propitiation" (AV). He explains: " . . . To appease an offended God. But if, as some teach, God never was offended, there was no need of this propitiation. And, if so, Christ died in vain."[5] The rules of God have been broken by sinners; God has been offended and must be appeased. At its second appearance (1 John 2:2), Wesley interprets this word "propitiation" to mean " . . . The atoning sacrifice by which the wrath of God is appeased". (At its third and final appearance, in 1 John 4:10, Wesley makes no comment at all.) This is ascribing to God human passions, and this we can only do "in an analogical sense" (Romans 5:9). To us this is how the atonement may appear to affect God. For certainly, if there is true forgiveness, there is no punishment for the offences. Thus the wrath of God appears to us to have been appeased.

But a further question must be asked: why does the death of Jesus have this result? The answer is also in Romans 3:25 – God set forth this propitiation:

> *To declare his righteousness* – To demonstrate not only His clemency [namely the forgiveness of sinners], but His justice; even that vindictive justice whose essential character and principal office is, to punish sin.

Wesley also uses the phrase "vindictive justice" at Romans 1:24, and "avenging justice" at Hebrews 10:31. The former was common in the eighteenth century and seems to mean retributive. It has not the spiteful meaning which it often bears today.[6] That this is true for Wesley may be deduced from the note on Romans 3:26: God is "strictly and inviolably righteous in the administration of His government . . . ". The atonement meets the requirements of justice. It is a "*demonstration of His righteousness* – Both of His justice and mercy". The righteousness of God means that he does what is right. This was "a real infliction of punishment on our Saviour". Thus, says Wesley, "the attribute of justice" is " preserved inviolate". The attribute of mercy is also preserved, justice having been done – "the sinner *that believeth in Jesus*" is now forgiven.

Wesley emphasises that Jesus suffered the punishment which justice metes out to sin (Romans 3:25). This bearing of punishment was the principle cause of his suffering:

> *He began to be sorrowful and in deep anguish* – Probably from feeling the arrows of the Almighty stick fast in his soul, while God 'laid on Him the iniquities of us all.' [Matthew 26:37; similarly at Matthew 27:45 f]

Christ's experience of forsakeness arose from, "His Father's withdrawing the tokens of His love, and treating Him as an enemy, while He bare our sins" (Mark 15:34; similarly Galatians 3:13). Christ was "content . . . to suffer the punishment, due to the meanest and vilest among them all" (Philippians 2:7). He suffered "the weight of infinite justice" (Hebrews 5:7) and the "punishment due" to sins (Hebrews 9:28). Wesley claims that only by the righteousness of our God and Saviour, Jesus Christ, is "the justice of God . . . satisfied" (2 Peter 1:1).

Beginning from Romans 3:24 f, probably the basic text in this matter, there seems to be no reasonable objection to the interpretation of the death of Jesus as a demonstration of the justice of God. Wesley makes clear again and again that the atonement is the work of the triune God, especially of Father and Son. The Father knows the Son and the Son the Father

"With such a knowledge as implies an inexpressible union" (John 10:15). In this union, Christ "cheerfully [sic!] die[s] to expiate the sins of men" (John 10:17). The justice of God demonstrated within such union becomes love, amazing love. In the words of Charles Wesley: "Amazing love! How can it be / That thou, my God, shouldst die for me!"[7]

However, Wesley goes further and equates the suffering of Jesus with the punishment due to all people for all sins, (Hebrews 9:14 and 28); it was a "ransom . . . more than equivalent" to such punishment (1 Timothy 2:6). This is questionable both as exegesis of the text and as application of justice. A ransom may not necessarily be equal to what the person ransomed is worth; it may be determined by what the holder wants. In this case, sinful people are held in custody awaiting sentence under the justice of God. The word ransom then becomes the price God pays within Himself as a demonstration of justice, even such justice which is also mercy, as the note on Romans 3:25 affirms. The death of Jesus is a ransom in the sense that as a result of His death people are set free in the court of God, "pardoned and accepted". Further, justice is not done if the punishment is "more than equivalent" to the retribution due to the offence. Indeed, Wesley undermines his comment by his introductory remark: " . . . Such a ransom, the word signifies, wherein a like or equal is given" (1 Timothy 2:6). It is illogical then to claim that this ransom was more than equivalent to what was needed. We may agree that this is the case, but the meaning lies not in the equivalence but in the effect. People are set free to come "*To the knowledge of the truth*" (1 Timothy 2:4).

The New Testament uses other terms to describe the death of Jesus; Wesley does not ignore these. The only occurrence of the term "atonement" in the AV, Wesley alters in his text to "reconciliation" (Romans 5:11), without comment, and in his note he simply repeats his translation, thereby emphasizing the effect of the death of Jesus, namely that He reconciles people to God by His death. This reconciling aspect of the atonement has been noted above with regard to other texts. Again, at 1 Peter 2:24, Wesley uses the term in his note: " . . . without an atonement first made for the guilt, we could never have been delivered from the power". Similarly, Jesus dies to expiate sin (John 10:17 and Hebrews 10:15). His death is an offering to God (Hebrews 9:14, 22, 23, 26 and 28). Neither at Mark 10:45 nor at Matthew 20:28 does Wesley comment on Christ's death as a ransom.

With regard to Christ's death as redemption, Wesley does not go beyond the interpretation at Romans 3:24: it is the "price Christ has paid" (also at Galatians 3:13). His death redeems the debt incurred by the sins of people (Colossians 2:14 and 1 John 1:9). Nowhere does he state that it was the price paid to God the Father, much less to the devil. The former idea may be implied; the latter does not enter the picture at all, because the need for atonement arises entirely from the relationship between God and people, broken by sin, described as "alienation" and "independency on God". The notes at Ephesians 1:7 and 14, where the word "redemption" occurs in the text, point to its effect on us and the change in our relationship with God. The note on Colossians 1:14 is a good summary of Wesley's understanding of the term 'redemption':

> The voluntary passion of our Lord appeased the Father's wrath, obtained pardon and acceptance for us, and, consequently, dissolved the dominion and power which Satan had over us through our sins. So that *forgiveness* is the beginning of redemption, as the resurrection is the completion of it. [For the latter thought, see note on 1 Corinthians 1:30.]

An aspect of the atonement which Wesley stresses in a long note on Romans 5 is the representative nature of Christ's death. This begins from the fact:

> *Christ died for the ungodly* . . . It does not appear that this expression . . . has any other signification than that of rescuing

the life of another by laying down our own. [verse 6]

Wesley contrasts the first Adam and the second, who is Jesus; the first brought sin, death, and the continuing power of sin (verse 14). Wesley describes the first Adam as "the common head and representative" of all sinners, and he continues:

So by the obedience of one – By His obedience unto death; by His dying for us. *Many* – All that believe. *Shall be constituted righteous* – Justified, pardoned. [verse 19]

Wesley implies a representative aspect of Christ's death, although he does not here apply the word directly to Him. He is representative of all who believe in Him, as dying for them. This thought is continued in Romans 6:3: " . . . In baptism we, through faith, are ingrafted into Christ . . . ". At 1 Corinthians 15:47, Wesley spells out clearly this implication:

As Adam was the first general representative of men, Christ was the second and the last. And what they severally did, terminated not in themselves, but affected all whom they represented.

This long examination of Wesley's interpretation of the death of Jesus may be concluded by returning to the starting point, Romans 3:24–6. Here, at verse 26, Wesley claims: "On this plan all the attributes harmonize; every attribute is glorified, and not one superseded, no, nor so much as clouded." At this point in the *Notes* the stress is on the two attributes of justice and mercy. This is true to Scripture at this point. However, it should not be overlooked that Wesley also attends to the goodness of God in the note on verse 24: "*Freely by his grace* . . . It is not possible to find words that . . . more emphatically ascribe the whole of our justification to free, unmerited goodness". The attributes of justice and mercy should not be allowed to blot out the attribute of goodness without which the atonement would not have been initiated. The goodness and love of God have been stressed in the sub-division above on the 'Initiative towards the Atonement.' Love is God's "darling, His reigning attribute". Unity is also an attribute of God. Thus, on Wesley's own terms, that all the attributes must harmonise, we must interpret justice, wrath and punishment within the whole range of attributes and each in the light of God's love which "sheds an amiable glory on all His other perfections" (1 John 4:8).

The Sinner's part in the Atonement

The atonement was made on account of sin and therefore for sinners. But sinners are "at a distance from God, alienated from Him, and incapable of a free access to Him"; they are in "total darkness, blindness, ignorance of God" (Matthew 1:16). Sinners are "inwardly and outwardly nothing but sin" (2 Corinthians 5:21); they are "Void of life" (1 John 5:19) and "totally enslaved" (Romans 7:14). Thus sinners have nothing to contribute to the act of atonement. Nevertheless, to make atonement effective for each person, each must show faith in God. The words "belief" and "faith" recur again and again in the texts and notes relevant to this chapter, eg at Colossians 1:21–2: "*He hath now reconciled* – From the moment ye believed . . . *Through death* – Whereby He purchased the reconciliation which we received by faith". For the sinner there can be no other part in the act of atonement. The atonement was made by Jesus in His death (see above). Sinners can only respond with trust in the adequacy of God's act in Christ (Matthew 15:28; Romans 4:9; 2 Corinthians 6:12; and Hebrews 11:1). On Romans 3:24, Wesley comments: "*Freely by his grace* . . . It is not possible to find words which should more absolutely exclude all consideration of our own works and obedience . . . ". There can only be faith on the part of sinners. But what kind of faith does Wesley envisage?

The quotation from Romans 3:24 supplies a clue to the answer to this question. "*Freely by his grace* – It is not possible to find words that should . . . more emphatically ascribe the whole of our justification to free, unmerited goodness." It is faith of the kind which responds not only to a demonstration of righteousness and justice by God, but also to his "free, unmerited goodness". The initiative in the atonement is God's entirely, and it is due to love, "His darling, His reigning attribute". Thus faith must be warm with love. Of his own experience Wesley wrote: " . . . I felt my heart strangely warmed. I felt I did trust in Christ, Christ alone for salvation".[8] Again, at Romans 5:1, love is one of the "fruits of justifying faith". Faith can be no other than warm with love towards God who so loved the sinner, for his goodness and love in the atonement. Thus for Wesley the faith which justifies is always "faith working by love", (Matthew 25:3; also Matthew 20:23; 24:31; 25:34; James 2:14 and especially 22; and Revelation 20:12). This combination of faith and love is the human aspect of the work of the Holy Spirit which begins with the gift of new life, making the sinner a new creation, and which ends with entire sanctification.

Summary

Because he is writing "explanatory notes on the New Testament," Wesley is here an interpreter of Scripture, not a systematic theologian. However, his notes on this doctrine may be drawn together as follows. The atonement is entirely the work of God, from initiative to completion and it is the work of God, Father, Son and Holy Spirit. In so far as the attributes of God are concerned, justice is done by the infliction of punishment on Jesus. This suffering is willingly faced, even prior to the incarnation, and is a "voluntary passion". This Son is in "inexpressible union" with the Father. Justice having been met, mercy can be exercised and pardon received, and so reconciliation takes place – such a reconciliation as unites the sinner to God the Father and God the Son by God the Holy Spirit, and produces a new life which culminates in eternity. The initiative towards the atonement is God's and this stems from his righteousness, which is a combination of justice and mercy. But while the throne of God speaks of power and justice, it is grace which "erected it and reigns there".

Some problems remain concealed within this interpretation. These must wait for attention in the final part of this examination of the *Notes*, under the general question: what is the meaning of accepting the *Notes* as a standard of doctrine if some details therein are unacceptable?

References

1 It is noteworthy that Wesley does not comment on the word propitiation in verse 10. The context concerns the love of Christians for one another (verse 7). Wesley rightly focuses on love rather than propitiation.

2 Cf "Vengeance is mine: I will repay" (Romans 12:19). "To me belongeth vengeance and recompense" (Deuteronomy 32:35). See also reference 6, below.

3 The Minutes of the early Conferences are extant and available in the libraries of Methodist Theological Colleges and elsewhere. Those of 1744–47 are quoted in Albert Outler's *John Wesley*, pp 134–76, in particular pp 151 and 163. The *Forty-four Standard Sermons* reflect the declarations about emphasising the wrath versus the love of God. There is no sermon on the wrath, nor on hell, although both are mentioned in various sermons. An example of both ideas is found in Sermon 3, 'Awake, Thou that Sleepest,' point I.:4:

> By one who sleeps, we are, therefore, to understand . . . one who never was warned, or never regarded the warning voice of God, 'to flee from the wrath to come'; one that never yet saw he was in danger of hell-fire . . .

4 At both Ephesians 2:15 and Colossians 2:14, Wesley "takes the liberty" to make a small alteration which changes the sense of the AV. He follows Bengel who translates the Greek "dogmasin" as "decrees" with respect to the mercy of God, and not as "ordinances" with respect to His Law. "These are the decrees of grace" (Bengel in Gnomon on Colossians 2:14). This finds no support in English versions nor in

English commentaries. However, the two notes may be allowed as evidence of Wesley's conviction that salvation is available to all.

5 Wesley seems to have written the note on this verse without drawing upon his main source. Cf Bengel: "The allusion to the mercy-seat . . . of the Old Testament" (Gnomon on Romans 3:25).

6 The Oxford English Dictionary gives some examples of the use of this phrase in the eighteenth century. Cowper wrote: "Pleasure brings as surely in her train / Remorse and Sorrow and vindictive pain." The phrase was common in that century. Retribution was the dominant element in the administration of justice, an infliction of the appropriate amount of pain, appropriate to the offence. This was determined at that time by an oligarchy bent upon protecting their property. In the case of divine justice which acts upon the throne of grace, we can be sure that the retributive element is perfectly appropriate to the offence.

7 Charles Wesley's hymn begins: "And can it be that I should gain . . . ". To be found in many hymnbooks. Hymns and Psalms 216, verse 1.

8 *Journal* Vol 1, p 476, 24 May 1738.

References to Scripture Texts

Matthew: 1:16; 3:15; 15:28; 25:3, 34; 26:37; 27:34, 45–46, 50

Mark: 10:38, 45; 14:33; 15:34

Luke: 22:44

John: 1:14, 18; 3:15–16; 8:28; 10:15, 17; 12:27; 14:19; 17:10, 19

Acts: 5:31; 20:28

Romans: 1:17, 24; 2:8; 3:20, 23–26, 28, 30; 4:5, 7, 9: 5:1, 5, 6, 8, 9, 11, 14, 16, 18–21; 6:3, 6, 10; 7:14; 8:3, 28–30, 33; 9:22, 30, 32

1 Corinthians: 1:30; 6:11; 15:47

2 Corinthians: 5:15, 19, 21; 8:32

Galatians: 3:13; 4:4

Ephesians: 1:7–11, 14; 2:16; 4:8

Philippians: 2:6–9

Colossians: 1:14, 21–33; 2:14–15

1 Timothy: 2:4–6

Titus: 2:14; 3:5

Hebrews: 2:9–10; 4:14, 16; 5:7–8; 8:12; 9:14–16, 22–23, 26,28; 10:7,
    9–10, 15; 11:1

James: 2:14, 22

1 Peter: 2:24

2 Peter: 1:1

1 John: 1:7, 9; 2:2; 4:8; 5:19

7

The Holy Spirit

T HE FIRST NOTE ON THE Holy Spirit seems an appropriate place to begin this doctrine.

He [Jesus] *shall baptize you with the Holy Ghost and with fire* – He shall fill you with the Holy Ghost, inflaming your hearts with that fire of love which many waters cannot quench. And this was done . . . on the day of Pentecost. [Matthew 3:11]

(1) The Holy Spirit produces love in the believer

. . . the love of God is shed abroad in our hearts – The divine conviction of God's love to us, and that love to God which is both the earnest and the beginning of heaven. *By the Holy Ghost* – The efficient cause of all these blessings, and the earnest of those to come. [Romans 5:5]

I beseech you by the love of the Spirit – That is, by the love which is the genuine fruit of the Spirit. [Romans 15:30 – This is the translation of the GNB; that of the REB is similar.]

In 1 Corinthians 12:1, Wesley presents a synopsis of chapters 12, 13 and 14.

Paul describes the unity of the body (verses 1–27); the variety of members and offices (verses 27–30); the way of exercising gifts rightly, by love (verse 31; 1 Corinthians 13:1–13), and adds a comparison of several gifts with each other (chapter 14).

We have all drunk of one Spirit . . . who first inspired, and still preserves, the life of God in our souls. [1 Corinthians 12:13 – "God is love", 1 John 4:8]

Ye covet earnestly the best gifts – And they are worth your pursuit, though but few of you can attain them. But there is a far more excellent gift than these; and one which all may, yea, must, attain or perish. [1 Corinthians 12:31]

In the preface to 1 Corinthians 13, Wesley notes that the "necessity of love is covered in verses 1–3. The nature and properties, verses 4–7. The duration of it, verses 8–13."

. . . *all we* that believe in Him, *beholding as in a glass* – In the mirror of the gospel – *The glory of the Lord* – His glorious love. *Are transformed into the same image* – Into the same love. *From* one degree of this *glory* to another, in a manner worthy of His almighty Spirit. [2 Corinthians 3:18]

But if ye are led by the Spirit – Of liberty and love, into all holiness. *Ye are not under the law* – Not under the curse or bondage of it; not under the guilt or the power of sin. [Galatians 5:18 – The justification of the first half of the note is to be found in the second half.]

Galatians 5:19–21 is a list of *"the works of the flesh"*. Wesley notes the plural:

Works are mentioned in the plural because they are distinct from, and often inconsistent with, each other. But 'the fruit of the Spirit' is mentioned in the singular, verse 22, as being all consistent and connected together. [Galatians 5:19]

Love – The root of all the rest. [Galatians 5:22]

. . . *sealed by that holy Spirit of promise* – Holy both in His nature and in His operations, and promised to all the children of God. The sealing seems to imply, (1) a full impression of the image of God on their souls; (2) a full assurance of receiving all the promises, whether relating to time or eternity. [Ephesians 1:13]

Your love in the Spirit – Your love wrought in you by the Spirit. [Colossians 1:8, GNB; REB is similar.]

Quench not the Spirit – Wherever it is, it burns; it flames in holy love, in joy, prayer, thanksgiving. [1 Thessalonians 5:19]

. . . for God hath not given us – That is, the spirit which God hath given us Christians, is not *the spirit of fear* – Or cowardice. *But of power* – Banishing fear. *And love, and sobriety* – These animate us in our duties to God, our brethren, and ourselves. *Power* and *sobriety* are two good extremes. *Love* is between, the tie and the temperament of both; preventing the two bad extremes of fearfulness and rashness. More is said concerning power, verse 8; concerning love, 2 Tim. ii. 14, &c.; concerning sobriety, 2 Tim. iii. 1, &c. [2 Timothy 1:7 – Wesley usually interprets in context, as these references show.]

. . . and the renewal of the Holy Ghost; which purifies the soul . . . and renews it in the whole image of God. [Titus 3:5]

Having purified your souls by obeying the truth through the Spirit, who bestows upon you freely, both obedience and purity of heart, and *unfeigned love of the brethren*, go on to still higher degrees of love. *Love one another fervently* – With the most strong and tender affection; and yet *with a pure heart* – Pure from any spot of unholy desire or inordinate passion. [1 Peter 1:22]

. . . live according to God in the Spirit. [AV]
. . . live according to the will and word of *God, in the Spirit*; the soul renewed after His image. [1 Peter 4:6]

The comma after "God", above, shows that Wesley is about to make a comment, not following the AV, as he is before the comma. The AV text is correct. Wesley is not altering it. But we cannot live according to the word and will of God unless we are in the Spirit. To live according to God's will and word is to have "the soul renewed after His image", and this is the work of the Holy Spirit.

. . . by the Spirit which he has given us – Which witnesses with our spirits that we are His children, and brings forth His fruits of peace, love, holiness. [1 John 3:24]

Let us love on another – From the doctrine he [John] has just been defending he draws this exhortation. It is by the Spirit that the love of God is shed abroad in our hearts. *Every one that* truly *loveth* God and his neighbour *is born of God.* [1 John 4:7]

The notes on 1 John 4:12–19 are printed in full because (a) they are relevant to our understanding of the Holy Spirit; (b) they demonstrate Wesley's principle of interpreting any part of Scripture in context; (c) they also demonstrate his conviction that "Scripture . . . is a most solid and precious system of divine truth . . . and an exactly regular series of arguments" (preface to the *Notes*, paragraphs 10–11).

If we love one another, God abideth in us – This is treated of, verses 13–6. *And his love is perfected* – Has its full effect. *In us* – This is treated of, verses 17–9. [verse 12]

And in consequence of this *we have seen and testify that the Father sent the Son* – These are the foundation and the criteria of our abiding in God and God in us – the communion of the Spirit, and the confession of the Son. [verse 14]

Whosoever shall, from a principle of loving faith, openly *confess* in the face of all opposition and danger, *that Jesus is the Son of God, God abideth in him*. [verse 15]

And we know and believe – By the same Spirit, *the love that God hath to us*. [verse 16]

Hereby – that is, by this communion with God. *Is our love made perfect, that we may* – That is, so that we shall *have boldness in the day of judgement* – When all the stout-hearted shall tremble. *Because as he* – Christ. *Is* – All love. *So are we* – Who are fathers in Christ, even *in this world.* [verse 17]

There is no fear in love – No slavish fear can be where love reigns. *But perfect*, adult *love casteth out* slavish *fear* : *because* such *fear hath torment* – And so is inconsistent with the happiness of love. A natural man has neither fear nor love; one that is awakened, fear without love; a babe in Christ, love and fear; a father in Christ, love without fear. [verse 18]

We love him, because he first loved us – This is the sum of all religion, the genuine model of Christianity. None can say more: why should anyone say less, or less intelligibly? [verse 19]

In verse 17 Wesley can assert that Christ "Is – All love" because God is love – 1 John 4:8. Hence the further assertion that this "is the sum of all religion" (verse 19). God first loved us and so we love Him. We are enabled to know and feel God's love by "the same Spirit" (verse 16).

This extended note and 20 others above show clearly Wesley's understanding of the main effect of the Holy Spirit in all believers:

. . . the [Holy] Spirit bearing witness [that we are true believers] by shedding the love of God abroad in your hearts, which is the highest testimony that can be given. [1 Thessalonians 1:5]

. . . *love unfeigned* [is] The chief fruit of the Spirit. [2 Corinthians 6:6]

(2) The Holy Spirit produces unity
Love produces unity. It unites, joining God to the world and people to God (John 3:16 and 1 John 4:10). It also joins believers to one another. This work of the Holy Spirit is emphasised in the notes (above) at 1 John 4:12–16 and also in

the following:

> *And this commandment have we from him* – both God and Christ. *That he who loveth God loves his brother* – Every one, whatever his opinions or mode of worship be, purely because he is the child, and bears the image of God. Bigotry is properly the want of this pure and universal love. A bigot only loves those who embrace his opinions, and receive his way of worship; and he loves them for that, and not for Christ's sake. [1 John 4:21]

> *Endeavouring to keep the unity of the Spirit* – That mutual union and harmony which is the fruit of the Spirit. *The bond of peace* is love. [Ephesians 4:3]

> *If there be therefore any consolation* – In the grace of Christ. *If any comfort* – In the love of God. I*f any fellowship of the* Holy Ghost; *if any bowels of mercies* – Resulting therefrom; any tender affection towards each other. [Philippians 2:1]

> *Think the same thing* – Seeing Christ is your common Head. *Having the same love* – To God, your common Father. *Being of one soul* – Animated with the same affections and tempers, as ye have all drunk into one spirit. *Of one mind* – Tenderly rejoicing and grieving together. [Philippians 2:2]

Wesley expects all Christians to be united by the Holy Spirit.

(3) The Holy Spirit is in all believers

This proposition is basic to the first point in this chapter (section 1). The Holy Spirit restores people to the image of God. The Holy Spirit must be in each in order to make this change. Wesley makes the point explicitly at the beginning of the story of the Church:

> *Ye shall be baptized with the Holy Ghost* – And so are all true believers, to the end of the world. [Acts 1:5]

The times of the Messiah are frequently called *the last days*, the gospel being the last dispensation of divine grace. *I will pour out of my spirit* – Not on the day of Pentecost only – *Upon all flesh* – On persons of every age, sex, and rank. *And your young men shall see visions* – In young men the outward senses are most vigorous, and the bodily strength is entire, whereby they are best qualified to sustain the shock which usually attends the visions of God. In old men the internal senses are most vigorous, suited to divine dreams. Not that the old are wholly excluded from the former, nor the young from the latter. [Acts 2:17]

And upon my servants – On those who are literally in a state of servitude. [Acts 2:18. Servants in the eighteenth century were often treated very cruelly. Wesley's note indicates that even these should be recipients of the Holy Spirit.]

The gift of the Holy Ghost does not mean, in this place, the power of speaking in tongues; for the promise of this was not given *to all that were afar off*, in distant ages and nations; but rather the constant fruits of faith, even righteousness, and peace, and joy in the Holy Ghost. [Acts 2:38]

The first comment arises from verse 39. Wesley is interpreting in context . The promise of sending the Holy Spirit (verse 33) comes from Joel 2:28, where it refers to the people of Judah when God lives on Mount Zion. Righteousness, peace and joy are the blessings of his reign. Joel makes no promise that people will speak in tongues.

The notes on Romans 8 proclaim Wesley's conviction that all believers are given the Holy Spirit – believers on the Lord Jesus as Paul has proclaimed him in chapters 3–7.

. . . *who walk . . . after the Spirit* – Who are guided in all our thoughts, words, and actions, not by corrupt nature, but by the Spirit of God. [Romans 8:4]

. . . they who are after the Spirit – Who are under His guidance. *Mind the things of the Spirit* – Think of, relish, love things invisible, eternal; the things which the Spirit hath revealed, which He works in us, moves us to, and promises to give us. [Romans 8:5]

In the Spirit – Under His government. *If any man have not the Spirit of Christ* – Dwelling and governing in him – *He is none of His* – He is not a member of Christ; not a Christian; not in a state of salvation. [Romans 8:9]

For as many as are led by the Spirit of God – In all the ways of righteousness. [Romans 8:14]

All Christians should be so led. "*That the righteousness of the law* – The holiness it required, described, verses 5–11." This is Wesley's note at the beginning of verse 4. It justifies the note at verse 14. Wesley is not plucking thoughts out of the air to suit his purpose.

In Romans 3–7, Paul sets forth the fundamental teaching of Christianity – salvation from sin, through faith in Jesus who died for all sinners, and the struggle between the old life dying in us and the new life growing in us, in each and every believer. As Paul states at Romans 5:5, the Holy Spirit is given to us.

Other notes which proclaim the same conviction include the following:

Now we have received, not the spirit of the world . . . But Christians receive the Spirit of God, which before they had not. [1 Corinthians 2:12]

Know ye not that ye are the temple of God, and the Spirit of God dwelleth in you? Ye – All Christians – *Are the temple of God*. [1 Corinthians 3:16]

And even your body . . . *is the temple of the Holy Ghost* – Dedicated to Him, and inhabited by Him. [1 Corinthians 6:19]

So no one can say, Jesus is the Lord – None can receive Him as such; for, in the scripture language, to say, or to believe, implies an experimental [experiential] assurance. *But by the Holy Ghost* – The sum is, None have the Holy Spirit but Christians; all Christians have this Spirit. [1 Corinthians 12:3]

If we live by the Spirit – If we are indeed raised from the dead, and are alive to God, by the operation of His Spirit. *Let us walk by the Spirit* – Let us follow His guidance, in all our tempers [attitudes], thoughts, words, and actions. [Galatians 5:25]

But he that soweth to the Spirit – That follows His guidance in all his tempers and conversation. *Shall of the Spirit* – By free grace and power of God, *reap life everlasting.* [Galatians 6:8]

The letter to the Galatians is directed to Christians who added circumcision to salvation by faith in the death of Jesus (2:19–20). Paul asks: did you receive the Holy Spirit by works or by faith at the time of hearing the message? He knows they received the Spirit at the time of hearing.

These notes on 1 Corinthians and Galatians affirm, explicitly or implicitly, that the Holy Spirit is in all believers. The Holy Spirit of promise is "promised to all the children of God" (Ephesians 1:13). He is "in the heart of every true believer" (Revelation 22:17).

(4) The Holy Spirit gives assurance to believers

The Holy Spirit is in all believers (Section 3 above). From this basic belief, Wesley develops the idea that assurance is given to believers by the Spirit:

The same Spirit beareth witness with our spirit – With the spirit of every true believer, by a testimony distinct from that of his own spirit, or the testimony of a good conscience. Happy they who enjoy this clear and constant! [Romans 8:16]

. . . no one can say, Jesus is the Lord – None can receive him as such; for, in the scripture language, to say, or to believe, implies an experimental (experiential) assurance. *But by the Holy Ghost* . . . all Christians have this Spirit. [1 Corinthians 12:3]

And because ye – Gentiles who believe, *are* also thus made His adult *sons, God hath sent forth the Spirit of his Son into your hearts* likewise, *crying, Abba, Father* – Enabling you to call upon God both with the confidence, and the tempers, of dutiful children. [Galatians 4:6]

. . . our gospel . . . came to you . . . with power and *With the Holy Ghost . . . With much assurance* – Literally, with *full assurance*, and *much* of it [NRSV, REB, NIV, JB translate – full/strong/deep/utter conviction – thus confirming Wesley's insight of the Greek.] . . . the Spirit bearing witness by shedding the love of God abroad in your hearts, which is the highest testimony that can be given. And these signs, if not the miraculous gifts, always attend the preaching of the gospel . . . [1 Thessalonians 1:5. For the meaning of "these signs" which are the Holy Spirit's witness in believers, see Romans 5:5 at section (1) above.]

To appreciate the note on Hebrews 6:11, the context should be kept in mind – verses 1–8. This is an appeal to Christians to "go on to perfection". It is also an appeal to those who have "*been made partakers of the Holy Ghost*" (verse 4). There is a danger that if they do not go on, they will go back (verses 4–6). The writer is confident of better things in their case, things that belong to salvation (verse 9). Because they are "partakers of the Holy Ghost", Wesley is justified in referring to the Holy Spirit in his note:

But we desire you may show the same diligence unto the end . . . To the full assurance of hope . . . The full assurance of faith relates to present pardon; the full assurance of hope, to future glory. The former is the highest degree of divine evidence that

91

God is reconciled to *me* in the Son of His love; the latter is the same degree of divine evidence (wrought in the soul by the same immediate inspiration of the Holy Ghost) of persevering grace, and of eternal glory. So much, and no more, as faith every moment 'beholds with open face,' so much does hope see to all eternity. But this assurance of faith and hope is not an opinion, not a bare construction of Scripture, but is given immediately by the power of the Holy Ghost; and what none can have for another, but for himself only.

. . . and hereby we know that he abideth in us, by the Spirit which he hath given us – Which witnesses with our spirits that we are His children, and brings forth His fruits of peace, love, holiness. [1 John 3:24]

The seven references above establish a Scriptural basis for the assurance which the Holy Spirit gives believers. It is given directly by the Spirit in a believer. But this is not the end of the matter. The verses from 2 Corinthians and 1 John include an external element alongside the direct assurance given by the Spirit; this is "the fruit of the Spirit". The reference to 1 Thessalonians draws attention to one of these – "love shed abroad in our hearts". Assurance is more that a 'feel good' factor in relation to God. If the Holy Spirit has no outward result in believers, the inner assurance is not genuine. The note at Galatians 4:6 draws attention to calling upon God with "the tempers [attitudes] of dutiful children". This reflects the parable of Jesus about the two sons who said the opposite to what they did – Matthew 21:28–31. Two other notes draw attention to the external accompaniment of the Spirit's assurance.

[After you had believed in Jesus] Ye were sealed by that holy Spirit of promise – Holy both in His nature and in His operations, and promised to all the children of God. The sealing seems to imply, (1) a full impression of the image of God on their souls; (2) a full assurance of receiving all the promises, whether relating to time or eternity. [Ephesians 1:13]

The image of God impressed on the soul of a believer should be noticeable by others. The promises of God which relate to life in this world are, for example, the fruit of the Spirit – visible to believer and non-believer (Galatians 5:22; Romans 6:1–14; 12:1–2; and Colossians 3:1–3, 10–19).

Grace be with you, mercy and peace, from God the Father and from Jesus Christ, the Son of the Father, in truth and love. Grace takes away guilt; *mercy* [takes away], misery: *peace* implies the abiding in grace and mercy. It includes the testimony of God's Spirit, both that we are His children, and that all our ways are acceptable to Him. This is the very foretaste of heaven itself, where it is perfected. [2 John 3]

(5) The Holy Spirit produces fruit in believers

The first effect of the Holy Spirit on believers is to inflame "your hearts with that fire of love" (Matthew 3:11), to produce "*love unfeigned*" (2 Corinthians 6:6) and ultimately "the soul renewed" in the image of God (1 Peter 4:6). The same emphasis is made at the following:

[The fruit of the Spirit is] *Love* – The root of all the rest. *Gentleness* – Toward all men; ignorant and wicked men in particular. *Goodness* – The Greek word means all that is benign, soft, winning, tender, either in temper or behaviour. [Galatians 5:22]

Meekness – Holding all the affections in even balance. [Galatians 5:23]

And they that are Christ's – True believers in Him – *Have* thus *crucified the flesh* – Nailed it, as it were, to a cross, whence it has no power to break loose, but is continually weaker and weaker. *With its affections and desires* – All its evil passions, appetites, and inclinations. [Galatians 5:24]

If we live by the Spirit – If we are indeed raised from the dead . . . by the operation of His Spirit. *Let us walk by the Spirit* – Let us follow His guidance, in all our tempers, thoughts, words, and actions. [Galatians 5:25]

The fruit of the light [Spirit] – Opposite to 'the unfruitful works of darkness' (verse 11). *Is in* – That is, consists in. *Goodness and righteousness and truth* – Opposite to the sins spoken of, Eph iv. 25, &c. [Ephesians 5:9]

. . . *be ye filled with the Spirit* – In all His graces, who gives a more noble pleasure than wine can do. [Ephesians 5:18. Wesley interprets both verses in the context of Ephesians 5, without any suggestion that these Christians needed a special experience of the Holy Spirit. Verse 19 continues this contextual interpretation.]

Speaking to each other – By the Spirit – *In* the *psalms* – Of David. *And hymns* – Of praise . . . On any divine subject. [Ephesians 5:19]

Fruit is what comes by nature from fruit trees. The nature of God is love (1 John 4:8). Therefore God the Holy Spirit in believers must produce love. Love includes unity, assurance, and the other virtues named above. These are the fruit of the Spirit, what the Spirit produces by His very nature, in all believers.

(6) The Holy Spirit gives abilities to believers to do God's work

Wesley writes the *Explanatory Notes* for those who "reverence and love the Word of God" and have "a desire to save their souls" (preface, paragraph 3). To read them for this purpose allows us to appreciate what Wesley says and guards us from expecting more from them than is necessary for this purpose. Why should we expect more?

The number of notes reflects the importance of this section of the Spirit's work for Wesley in Christian work of his day. It is equally important today. The followers of John Wesley ought to know what he says on the subject of "gifts of the Spirit".

And they began to speak with other tongues – The miracle was not in the ears of the hearers (as some have unaccountably supposed), but in the mouth of the speakers. And this family praising God together, with the tongues of all the world, was an earnest that the whole world should in due time praise God in their various tongues. – *As the Spirit gave them utterance* – Moses, the type of the law, was of a slow tongue; but the gospel speaks with a fiery and flaming one. [Acts 2:4]

Wesley claims to interpret Scripture by Scripture. His reference to the whole world praising God is justified by Philippians 2:11. This praise is a foretaste of the objective of the age of grace, offered to all at Pentecost. For Acts 2:38, see under section 3 of this chapter.

Full of the Holy Ghost and wisdom – For it is not a light matter to dispense even the temporal goods of the Church. To do even this well, a large measure both of the gifts and grace of God is requisite [required]. [Acts 6:3]

How God anointed Jesus – Particularly at His baptism, thereby inaugurating Him to His office – *With the Holy Ghost and with power* – It is worthy our remark that frequently when the Holy Ghost is mentioned there is added a word particularly adapted to the present circumstance. So the deacons were to be '*full of the Holy Ghost and wisdom*' (Acts vi 3) . . . and here, where His mighty works are mentioned, Christ Himself is said to be *anointed with the Holy Ghost and with power*. [Acts 10:38]

The Holy Ghost fell on all that were hearing the word – Thus were they consecrated to God, as the first-fruits of the Gentiles. And thus did God give a clear and satisfactory evidence that He had accepted them as well as the Jews. [Acts 10:44. Wesley's note points to the uniqueness of the occasion.]

In Acts 10:47, Wesley's note is directed entirely to baptism (see chapter 9, below):

God bare them witness – That He had accepted them by giving them the Holy Ghost. [Acts 15:8. Wesley does not go any further than the Scripture goes.]

Have ye received the Holy Ghost – The extraordinary gifts of the Spirit, as well as His sanctifying graces? *We have not so much as heard* – Whether there be any such gifts. [Acts 19:2]

The above note seems to be written in the light of verse 6 – "*spake with tongues, and prophesied*". Wesley makes no reference to these, nor does he speculate as to why Paul asked the question of verse 2. He concentrates on the main point, namely the baptism of John for repentance. The difference between this and the baptism in the name of Jesus is demonstrated by the gifts of tongues and prophecy. These were the gifts bestowed on the Apostles on the day of Pentecost – prophecy in the sense of proclaiming the message of God. These gifts were bestowed on the first Gentiles before baptism, thus showing God's acceptance of them also (10:44–46). This was a unique occasion, a break-through into the Gentile world. The Ethiopian of Acts 8 was already a convert to Judaism. At Acts 19 the gifts – verse 6 – show that baptism "*in the name of the Lord Jesus*" is much more than the baptism of John. This event is also a unique incident. As Wesley comments: " . . . the whole baptism and preaching of John pointed at Christ" (verse 4).

. . . the flock, over which the Holy Spirit has made you overseers – For no man or number of men upon earth can constitute an overseer, bishop, or any other Christian minister. To do this is

the peculiar work of the Holy Ghost. [Acts 20:28]

This is the final reference in Acts to a gift made by the Holy Spirit; it points us to the gifts listed in Romans 12, 1 Corinthians 12–14 and Ephesians 4.

Romans 12:3–8 make no reference to the Holy Spirit, nor does Wesley in the notes thereon. For example, in Romans 12:3 he comments that God has distributed to everyone the measure of faith "from which all other gifts and graces flow". In this context, God means the Father.

In 1 Corinthians 12:14, the gifts come through the Holy Spirit; in Ephesians 4:11–13, the gifts are distributed by Christ ascended. The three origins of the gifts are reconcilable in the doctrine of the Trinity.

The notes which name the Holy Spirit are a small portion of the total in 1 Corinthians 12–14. They are given below, along with Wesley's interpretation of the gifts.

... None have the Holy Spirit but Christians: all Christians have this Spirit. [1 Corinthians 12:3]

There are diversities of gifts, but the same Spirit – Divers streams, but all from one fountain. [1 Corinthians 12:4]

The manifestation – The gift whereby the Spirit manifests itself. *Is given to each* – For the profit of the whole body. [1 Corinthians 12:7]

The word of wisdom – A power of understanding and explaining the manifold wisdom of God in the grand scheme of gospel salvation. *The word of knowledge* – Perhaps an extraordinary ability to understand and explain the Old Testament types and prophecies. [1 Corinthians 12:8]

Faith may here mean an extraordinary trust in God under the most difficult or dangerous circumstances. *The gift of healing* need not be wholly confined to healing diseases with a word or touch. It may exert itself also, though in a lower degree, where natural remedies are applied; and it may often be this, not superior skill, which makes some physicians more successful than others . . . after the pure gifts are lost, the power of God exerts itself in a more covert manner, under human studies and helps; and that the more plentifully, according as there is the more room given for it. [1 Corinthians 12:9]

Prophecy – Foretelling things to come. *The discerning of spirits* – Whether men be of an upright spirit or no; whether they have natural or supernatural gifts for offices in the Church; and whether they who profess to speak by inspiration speak from a divine, a natural, or a diabolical spirit. [1 Corinthians 12:10]

Wesley is thoroughly practical in his interpretation of these gifts of the Spirit. His understanding of them is a good foundation, standing on which we can examine ourselves, or others, with regard to the gifts of the Spirit.

We have all drunk of one Spirit – In that cup, received by faith, we all imbibed *one Spirit*, who first inspired, and still preserves, the life of God in our souls. [1 Corinthians 12:13. This is the standard by which the working of the various gifts is to be measured. For "that cup" see 1 Corinthians 10:16–17.]

Ye covet earnestly the best gifts – And they are worth your pursuit, though but few of you can attain them. But there is a far more excellent gift than all these; and one which all may, yea, must, attain or perish. [1 Corinthians 12:31]

The above is emphasised by the notes on 1 Corinthians 13:1–3. Some of these notes appear in chapter 12, 'Practical Christianity'. Wesley concludes:

And have not the *love* – Hereafter described. *It profiteth me nothing* – Without this [love], whatever I speak, whatever I have, whatever I know, whatever I do, whatever I suffer, is nothing. [verse 3]

The importance of Love is shown by the length of the notes on chapter 13, even though it has nothing difficult to understand. They are twice as long as those on chapter 12, in proportion to the number of verses in each chapter.

If I pray in an unknown tongue . . . My spirit prayeth – By the power of the Spirit I understand the words myself. *But my understanding is unfruitful* – The knowledge I have is no benefit to others. [1 Corinthians 14:14]

I will pray with the Spirit, but I will pray with the understanding also – I will use my own understanding, as well as the power of the Spirit. I will not act so absurdly, as to utter in a congregation what can edify none but myself. [1 Corinthians 14:15]

Wesley experienced this gift of the Spirit in some of his listeners (see Rack, *Reasonable Enthusiast*, pp 187 and 195). The *Notes on the New Testament* are written out of his experience of proclaiming the Gospel.

But in understanding be ye grown men – Knowing religion was not designed to destroy any of our natural faculties, but to exalt and improve them, our reason is particular. [1 Corinthians 14:20]

For our gospel came . . . to you . . . with power, and with the Holy Ghost . . . the Spirit bearing witness by shedding the love of God abroad in your hearts, which is the highest testimony that can be given. And these signs, if not the miraculous gifts, always attend the preaching of the gospel . . . [1 Thessalonians 1:5]

The signs are named in 1 Thessalonians 1:3 where Wesley comments:

Your work of faith – Your active, ever-working faith. *And labour of love* – Love continually labouring for the bodies or souls of men. They, who do not thus labour, do not love. *Faith* works, *love* labours, *hope* patiently suffers all things.

. . . *preached the gospel to you with the Holy Ghost* . . . Confirmed by the inward, powerful testimony of the Holy Ghost, as well as the mighty effusion of His miraculous gifts. [1 Peter 1:12]

(7) Some Problem Statements

The blasphemy against the Spirit – How much stir has been made about this! How many sermons, yea, volumes, have been written concerning it! And yet there is nothing plainer in the Bible. It is neither more nor less than the ascribing those miracles to the power of the devil which Christ wrought by the power of the Holy Ghost. [Matthew 12:31]

Whosoever speaks against the Son of man – In any other respect. *It shall be forgiven him* – Upon his true repentance. *But whosoever speaketh* thus *against the Holy Ghost, it shall not be forgiven, neither in this world, nor in the world to come* – This was a proverbial expression among the Jews for a thing that would never be done. It here means, further, he shall not escape the punishment of it either in this world on in the world to come. The judgement of God shall overtake him both here and hereafter. [Matthew 12:32]

How easily may a man of learning elude the strongest proof of a work of God! How readily can he account for every incident, without ever taking God into question! [Mark 3:22]

Because they said, He hath an unclean spirit – Is it not astonishing that men who have ever read these words should doubt what is the blasphemy against the Holy Ghost? Can any words declare more plainly that it is 'the ascribing those miracles to the power of the devil which Christ wrought by the power of the Holy Ghost"? [Mark 3:30]

And whosoever – As if He had said, Yet the denying Me in some degree may, upon true repentance, be forgiven; but if it rise so high as that of the blasphemy against the Holy Ghost, it shall never be forgiven, neither is there place for repentance. [Luke 12:10. It should be noted that the context in Luke is a teaching section; in Matthew and Mark, the sentences occur in an argument with the Pharisees.]

It is impossible for those who were once enlightened – With the light of the glorious love of God in Christ. *And have tasted the heavenly gift* – Remission of sins, sweeter than honey and the honeycomb. *And been made partakers of the Holy Ghost* – Of the witness and the fruit of the Spirit. [Hebrews 6:4]

And have tasted the good word of God – Have had a relish for and a delight in it. *And the powers of the world to come* – Which every one tastes who has a hope full of immortality. Every child that is naturally born first sees the light, then receives and tastes proper nourishment, and partakes of the things of this world. In like manner, the apostle, comparing spiritual with natural things, speaks of one born of the Spirit, as seeing the light, tasting the sweetness, and partaking 'of the world to come.' [Hebrews 6:5]

And have fallen away – Here is not a supposition, but a plain relation of fact. The apostle here describes the case of those who have cast away both the power and the form of godliness; who have lost both their faith, hope, and love (verse 10 &c.), and that wilfully (Heb. x. 26). Of these wilful total apostates he declares, *it is impossible to renew them again to repentance* (though they were renewed once), either to the foundation, or anything built thereon. *Seeing they crucify the Son of God afresh* – They use Him with the utmost indignity. *And put him to an open shame* – Causing His glorious name to be blasphemed. [Hebrews 6:6]

But, beloved – In this one place he calls them so. He never uses

101

this appellation but in exhorting. *We are persuaded of you things that accompany salvation* – We are persuaded you are now saved from your sins; and that ye have faith, love, and holiness, which lead to final salvation. *Though we thus speak* – To warn you, lest you should fall from your present steadfastness. [Hebrews 6:9]

These notes on Hebrews 6:4, 5, 6 and 9 should be studied as a whole before applying any sentence either of the Scripture or of the notes to a particular person. Wesley correctly understands verse 6 as a warning. The readers have not reached this stage (note verse 9).

Wesley does not soften any of these difficult verses of Scripture. But, as the notes on Hebrews 6 demonstrate, it is essential to examine if a person spoke against the Holy Spirit, and if s/he was speaking wilfully, not through ignorance, and not under persecution.

(8) Methods of Working

... *the Spirit of God* [descending] ... in the shape of a dove ... This was a visible token of those secret operations of the blessed Spirit, by which He [Jesus] was anointed in a peculiar manner, and abundantly fitted for His public work. [Matthew 3:16]

Then [Jesus was led] ... *By the Spirit* – Probably through a strong inward impulse. [Matthew 4:1]

These two notes set the tone for all the notes which touch on the method by which the Holy Spirit works in believers. Wesley has little more to say, as is demonstrated by the note on John 3:8: "*So is everyone that is born of the Spirit* – The fact is plain; the manner of His operations, inexplicable."

In brief summary, the phrases used are: "impulse" (Luke 2:27); "strongly impelled" (Acts 20:22); "inward dictate" (Acts

16:6); "inward, powerful testimony" (1 Peter 1:12); "strong impression" (Acts 16:7); and "His motions" (Hebrews 10:29). At 1 Corinthians 2:4, the Holy Spirit "works on the conscience with the most convincing light, and the most persuasive evidence". And at Acts 18:5:

Paul was pressed in spirit . . . Every Christian ought diligently to observe any such pressure in his own spirit, and, if it agree with the Scripture, to follow it: if he does not, he will feel great heaviness.

The note in 1 Corinthians is in the context of preaching Christ crucified. The Holy Spirit then works on the conscience of people.

The note on Acts 18 declares that the inward dictate must be in agreement with Scripture. This guideline is especially relevant now when so much emphasis is placed on the work of the Holy Spirit.

The gentle nature of the work of the Holy Spirit, as a dove, appears in the following notes:

And the child [Jesus] *grew* . . . *And waxed strong in spirit* . . . *Filled with wisdom* – By the light of the indwelling Spirit, which gradually opened itself in His soul. [Luke 2:40]

[While Peter was musing on the vision, the Spirit said to him] How gradually was St. Peter prepared to receive this new admonition of the Spirit! Thus God is wont to lead on His children by degrees, always giving them light for the present hour. [Acts 10:19]

In the case of Jesus, the Holy Spirit could only work gradually in the child. His mind could not grasp then what he understood later about, for example, his death. In the case of Peter, God led him gently across the gap between Jew and Gentile. The Holy Spirit sometimes works gradually in a believer.

8
The Trinity

(1) The Godhead of the Holy Spirit

THE GODHEAD OF JESUS IN the *Notes on the New Testament* has been demonstrated in Chapter 3, 'Christology.' The Godhead of the Holy Spirit must be shown before proceeding to the doctrine of the Trinity.

And that which is born of the Spirit is spirit – Is spiritual, heavenly, divine, like its Author. [John 3:6. Namely the Spirit.]

When the Comforter is come, whom will I send to you from the Father, the Spirit of truth, who proceedeth from the Father, he shall testify of me – The Spirit's coming, and being sent by our Lord from the Father, to testify of Him, are personal characters, and plainly distinguish Him from the Father and the Son; and His title as *the Spirit of truth*, together with His proceeding from the Father, can agree to none but a divine person. [John 15:26]

Thou hast not lied to men only, *but to God* also. Hence the Godhead of the Holy Ghost evidently appears; since lying to Him (verse 3) is lying to God. [Acts 5:4]

. . . your body . . . *is the temple of the Holy Ghost* – Dedicated to Him, and inhabited by Him. What the apostle calls elsewhere 'The temple of God' (1 Cor. iii. 16, 17) . . . he here styles *the temple of the Holy Ghost*; plainly showing that the Holy Ghost is the living God. [1 Corinthians 6:19]

. . . *because the Spirit is truth* – The very God of truth. [1 John 5:6]

The Godhead of the Holy Spirit appears in each of these notes, distinct in itself. The notes on the Trinity (below) affirm or imply the divinity of the Spirit. For Wesley, that he is God does not depend on the above notes only.

(2) Trinity – Father, Son and Holy Spirit

The following notes demonstrate Wesley's firm belief in the Trinity and its importance in Christian discipleship.

And lo, a voice – We have here a glorious manifestation of the ever-blessed Trinity: the Father speaking from heaven, the Son spoken to, the Holy Ghost descending upon Him. [Matthew 3:17. As early as this in the *Notes*, Wesley declares the centrality of the Trinity in Christian thought.]

The Lord our God is one Lord . . . one God, essentially, though three persons. From this unity of God it follows that we owe all our love to Him alone. [Mark 12:29]

He [John] *shall be great before the Lord* – God the Father. Of the Holy Ghost and the Son of God mention is made immediately after. [Luke 1:15]

The Holy Ghost shall come upon thee, and the power of the Highest shall overshadow thee – The power of God was put forth by the Holy Ghost, as the immediate divine agent in this work; and so He exerted the power of the Highest as His own power, who, together with the Father and the Son, is the Most High God. [Luke 1:35]

He [God] *hath anointed me* – With the spirit . . . How is the doctrine of the ever-blessed Trinity interwoven even in those scriptures where one would least expect it! How clear a declaration of the great Three-One is there in these very words, 'The *Spirit* of the *Lord* is upon *me*.' [Luke 4:18]

. . . *how would ye believe if I told you heavenly things?* – Such as the eternity of the Son; and the unity of the Father, Son, and Spirit. [John 3:12. Of all the heavenly things which Jesus might have told his audience that evening, Wesley chose two examples: the first relates to the Trinity; the second explicitly affirms it.]

It is expedient for you – In respect of the Comforter (verse 7, &c.), and of Me (verse 16, &c.), and of the Father (verse 23, &c.). [John 16:7. Wesley interprets this chapter as an explicit affirmation of the Trinity.]

Repent – And hereby return to God. *Be baptized, believing in the name of Jesus, and ye shall receive the gift of the Holy Ghost* – See the Three-One God clearly proved. [Acts 2:38]

In the name of the Lord – Which implies the Father who anointed Him, and the Spirit with which He was anointed, to His office. [Acts 10:48]

The Lord of glory – The giving Christ this august title, peculiar to the great Jehovah, plainly shows Him to be the supreme God. In like manner the Father is styled, 'the Father of glory'(Eph. i. 17); and the Holy Ghost, 'the spirit of glory' (1 Pet. iv. 14). The application of this title to all the three shows that the Father, Son, and Holy Ghost are 'the God of glory'; as the only true God is called (Ps. xxix. 3, and Acts vii. 2). [1 Corinthians 2:8]

This verse speaks of the Holy Ghost, the next of Christ, the sixth of God the Father. The apostle treats of the Spirit, verses 7 &c.; of Christ, verses 12 &c.; of God, verses 28 &c. [1 Corinthians 12:4. Again Wesley points to a Trinitarian pattern in the structure of the teaching.]

For through him we both have access – Liberty of approaching, *by* the guidance and aid of *one spirit to* God as our *Father*. Christ, the Spirit, and the Father, the three-one God, stand frequently in the same order. [Ephesians 2:18]

If there be therefore any consolation – In the grace of Christ. *If any comfort* – In the love of God. *If any fellowship* . . . [in the]

Holy Ghost; *if any bowels of mercies* – Resulting therefrom; any tender affection towards each other. [Philippians 2:1]

Wesley sees the pattern of the Trinity in phrases 1, 2 and 3. Grace, love and fellowship from God the Father, Son and Holy Spirit should produce "tender affection towards each other". Wesley retains the AV translation, but he gives his own in the note. Here, he anticipates some twentieth-century English translations. Wesley's insight that the phrases reflect the Trinity is supported by JB: "almost certainly meant to be taken as a Trinitarian reference".

Praying through the Holy Spirit – Who alone is able to build you up, as He alone laid the foundation. In this and the following verse St. Jude mentions the Father, Son, and Spirit, together with faith, love, and hope. [Jude 20]

The titles given our Lord . . . in the four latter, [letters, show respect for] His divine glory, and unity with the Father and the Holy Spirit. [Revelation 3:22]

Wesley finds "the ever blessed Trinity even in those Scriptures where one would least expect it". Before dismissing some of the above references to the Trinity, it is instructive to examine a note in which the reference to the Trinity at first sight seems to be Wesley's own idea.

That . . . you may walk worthy of the Lord, unto all pleasing – So as actually to please Him in all things; daily *increasing in the* living, experimental [experiential] *knowledge of God*, our Father, Saviour, Sanctifier. [Colossians 1:10]

They are to increase in the knowledge of God who has been described in verses 3–8: "*the God and father of our Lord Jesus Christ*", "*your faith in Christ Jesus*" (as Saviour), "*Your love in the Spirit*". God, Father, Son and Holy Ghost, is the essence of the message in these verses. The Colossians are to increase in the knowledge of this three-one God.

> *There is one body* – The universal Church, all believers throughout the world. *One Spirit, One Lord, One God and Fathe*r – The ever-blessed Trinity. [Ephesians 4:4]

At the end of the twentieth century this understanding of God is as relevant as it was in the eighteenth and in the first centuries.

(3) The Lord Jesus and the Holy Spirit

The terms Father and Son relate these persons of the Trinity to each other. They rebuke us if we ever begin to separate these persons in our thinking or praying. The following notes remind us that the New Testament also links the Holy Spirit and the Lord Jesus.

> *The Spirit of truth* – Who has, reveals, testifies, and defends the truth as it is in Jesus. [John 14:17]

> *. . . the Holy Ghost, whom the Father will send in My name* – For My sake, in My room as My agent. *He will teach you all things* – Necessary for you to know. Here is a clear promise to the apostles and their successors in the faith, that the Holy Ghost will teach them all that truth which is needful for their salvation. [John 14:26]

> And that He [the Holy Spirit] proceeds from the Son, as well as from the Father, may be fairly argued from His being called 'the Spirit of Christ' (1 Pet. i. 11), and from His being here said to be sent by Christ from the Father, as well as sent by the Father in his name. [John 15:26]

> *But they who are after the Spirit* – Who are under His guidance. *Mind the things of the Spirit* – Think of, relish, love things invisible, eternal; the things which the Spirit has revealed, which He works in us, moves us to, and promises to give us. [Romans

8:5. This verse and Wesley's note on it can only be applied to the Holy Spirit.]

[You are] *In the Spirit* – Under His government ["guidance" at verse 5]. *If any man have not the Spirit of Christ* – Dwelling and governing in him ["the things which the Spirit moves us to" at verse 5 – Here again Wesley understands "the Spirit" to be the Holy Spirit.]. [Romans 8:9]

Now if Christ be in you – Where the Spirit of Christ is, there is Christ. [Romans 8:10]

This last note makes sense only if the Spirit of Christ means the Holy Spirit. He is the Spirit, which Christ sends. By writing "the Spirit of Christ", Paul has emphasised the bond between the Holy Spirit and the Lord Jesus. Wesley's note is a further emphasising of the bond.

How much more shall the blood of Christ, who through the eternal Spirit offered Himself without spot to God – The work of redemption being the work of the whole Trinity. Neither is the Second person alone concerned even in the amazing condescension that was needful to complete it. The Father delivers up the kingdom to the Son; and the Holy Ghost becomes the gift of the Messiah, being, as it were, sent according to His good pleasure. [Hebrews 9:14]

These notes link the Holy Spirit to Jesus, and also to God the Father. This link, which is implicit in the concept of the Trinity, should help believers to test claims that the Holy Spirit directed an action or sent a message. The Trinity is the three-one God. It is not a verbal disguise for three Gods who make up the Godhead.

(4) The Importance of the Doctrine

This review of the notes which refer to the Trinity, shows how important Wesley considered this doctrine to be. The Dissenting *a little harsh.* ?

Academies, because they encouraged freethinking, tended towards heresy and theological anarchy in Wesley's time. In the present time, the Godhead of the Lord Jesus and of the Holy Spirit is accepted by the vast majority of believers. However, frequently it seems that Father, Son and Holy Spirit each has a part to play in the life of the believer, but with little connection between them. The note at Ephesians 4:6 affirms: "*One God and Father of all* – That believe. *Who is above all* – Presiding over all His children, operating through them *all* by Christ, *and* dwelling *in all* by His Spirit." Such a reading of Scripture is valuable today and always.

John Wesley sets a very high standard for Methodist theology concerning the Trinity, and for discipleship flowing from this theology. Charles Wesley expresses this in a couplet from a hymn:

You, whom God ordained to be
Transcripts of the Trinity.

9
The Sacraments

WESLEY ADHERED TO THE TWO sacraments affirmed in Article 25 of the Church of England's Articles of Religion. He included both in his sermon on 'The Means of Grace,' and administered both to the end of his life. His review of his life before 24 May 1738 provides an insight into his understanding of the Sacraments. It is given below in the very condensed form, in his own words, so that readers may assess for themselves what light it throws on his understanding of the Sacraments:

> I believe, till I was almost ten years old, I had not sinned away 'the washing of the Holy Ghost' which was given to me in baptism . . . Being removed to the University for five years, I still said my prayers and read, with the Scriptures, several other books of religion, especially comments on the New Testament. Yet I had not all this while as much as a notion of inward holiness.

Wesley read William Law's *Christian Perfection* and *A Serious Call to a Devout and Holy Life*, along with other books. The result was as follows:

> By my continued endeavour to keep his whole law, inward and outward, to the utmost of my power, I was persuaded that I should be accepted of Him (Christ), that I was even then in a state of salvation . . . Diligently I strove against all sin . . . I carefully used, both in public and in private, all the means of grace at all opportunities. I omitted no occasion of doing good . . . Yet . . . I could not find that all this gave me . . . any assurance of acceptance with God.

Wesley found this assurance in a direct experience of God on that evening in May in a meeting of Christians in London.

Baptism

On board ship (1735), Wesley baptised "Thomas Hird and Grace, his wife, their children, Mark aged 21 and Phoebe, about 17, who had been educated among the Quakers". The *Journal* records other adult baptisms up to 1785. In Savannah, Wesley "baptized Mary Welch, 11 days old". He "christened" children on three occasions in 1789 and 1790. His practice is clear to the end of his life.

What meaning do the *Notes on the New Testament* give to these baptisms?

(1) Baptism is a command of the Lord Jesus

Go ye, and disciple all nations, baptizing them in the name of the Father, and of the Son, and of the Holy Ghost. Disciple all nations – Make them My disciples. This includes the whole design of Christ's commission. Baptizing and teaching are the two great branches of that general design. And these were to be determined by the circumstances of things; which made it necessary, in baptizing adult Jews or heathens, to teach them before they were baptized; in discipling their children, to baptize them before they were taught: as the Jewish children, in all ages, were first circumcised, and after taught to do all God had commanded them. [Matthew 28:19]

He that believeth and is baptized shall be saved; but he that believeth not shall be damned. And is baptized – In token thereof [of his believing]. Everyone that believed was baptized. *But he that believeth not* – Whether baptized or unbaptized, shall perish everlastingly. [Mark 16:16]

Can any man forbid water, that these should not be baptized, who have received the Holy Ghost? – He [Paul] does not say, They have the baptism of the Spirit; therefore they do not need baptism with water: but just the contrary; If they have received the Spirit, then baptize them with water.

How easily is this question decided, if we will take the Word of God for our judge! Either men have received the Holy Ghost, or not. If they have not, 'Repent,' saith God, 'and be baptized, and ye shall receive the gift of the Holy Ghost.' If they have, if they are already baptized with the Holy Ghost, then, *who can forbid water?* [Acts 10:47]

(2) Baptism is a sign, not an act of magic

. . . he that believeth not – Whether baptized or unbaptized, shall perish everlastingly. [Mark 16:16]

That he might sanctify it through the word – The ordinary channel of all blessings. *Having cleansed it* – From the guilt and power of sin. *By the washing of water* – In baptism; if, with 'the outward and visible sign,' we receive the 'inward and spiritual grace.' [Ephesians 5:26]

The antitype whereof – The thing typified by the ark, even *baptism, now saveth us* – That is, through the water of baptism we are saved from the sin which overwhelms the world as a flood: *not*, indeed, the bare outward sign, but the inward grace; a divine consciousness that both our persons and our actions are accepted through Him who died and rose again for us. [1 Peter 3:21]

(3) The sign of baptism is linked to the thing signified

Except a man be born of water and of the Spirit – Except he experience that great inward change by the Spirit, and be baptized (wherever baptism can be had), as the outward sign and means of it. [John 3:5. The inward change is the cleansing "from the guilt and power", as at Ephesians 5:26.]

Be baptized, and wash away thy sins – Baptism, administered to real penitents, is both a means and seal of pardon. Nor did God ordinarily in the primitive Church bestow this on any, unless

113

through this means. [Acts 22:16]

For by that one Spirit, which we received in baptism, we are all united in one body. *Whether Jews or Gentiles* – Who are at the greatest distance from each other by nature. *Whether slaves or freemen* – Who are at the greatest distance by law and custom. *We have all drunk of one Spirit* – In that cup, received by faith, we all imbibed *one Spirit*, who first inspired, and still preserves, the life of God in our souls. [1 Corinthians 12:13]

. . . *buried with him in baptism* . . . but only on our being risen with Christ, through the powerful operation of God in the soul; which we cannot but know assuredly, if it really is so: and if we do not experience this, our baptism has not answered the end of its institution. [Colossians 2:12]

Not by works – In this important passage the apostle presents us with a delightful view of our redemption. Herein we have, (1) The cause of it; not our *works* or *righteousness*, but 'the kindness and love of God our Saviour.' (2) The effects; which are, (a) Justification; 'being justified,' pardoned and accepted through the alone merits of Christ, not from any desert in us, but *according to his own mercy*, 'by his grace,' His free, unmerited goodness: (b) sanctification, expressed by *the laver of regeneration*, (that is, baptism, the thing signified, as well as the outward sign), *and the renewal of the Holy Ghost*; which purifies the soul, as water cleanses the body, and renews it in the whole image of God. (3) The consummation of all – *that we might become heirs of eternal life*, and live now in the joyful hope of it. [Titus 3:5]

(4) Baptism is Trinitarian

. . . *to be baptized in the name of the Lord* – Which implies the Father who anointed Him, and the Spirit with which He was anointed, to His office. But as these Gentiles had before believed in God the Father, and could not but now believe in the

Holy Ghost, under whose powerful influence they were at this very time, there was the less need of taking notice that they were baptized into the belief and profession of the sacred Three; though doubtless the apostle administered the ordinance in that very form which Christ Himself had prescribed. (Acts 10:48. See also Matthew 28:19.]

And hearing this they were baptized – By some other. *Paul only laid his hands upon them. They were baptized* – They were baptized twice; but not with the same baptism. John did not administer that baptism which Christ afterwards commanded; that is, in the name of the Father, Son, and Holy Ghost. [Acts 19:5]

(5) Baptism is administered to adults who have faith and repentance

This is made clear in the notes at Matthew 28:19; Acts 10:48; 1 Corinthians 12:13; Mark 16:16; Acts 22:16; Ephesians 5:26; John 3:5; and Colossians 2:12.

Circumcision indeed profiteth – He does not say, justifies. How far it profited is shown in the third and fourth chapters. *Thy circumcision is become uncircumcision* – Is so already in effect. Thou wilt have no more benefit by it than if thou hadst never received it. The very same observation holds with regard to baptism. [Romans 2:25. Wesley views the baptism of infants as the Christian counterpart of circumcision under the covenant made with Abraham. See note above on Matthew 28:19.]

As many as have been baptized into Christ Jesus have been baptized into his death – In baptism we, through faith, are ingrafted into Christ; and we draw new spiritual life from this new root, through His Spirit, who fashions us like unto Him, and particularly with regard to His death and resurrection. [Romans 6:3]

We are buried with him – Alluding to the ancient manner of baptizing by immersion. *That as Christ was raised from the dead by the glory* – Glorious power. *Of the Father, so we also*, by the same power, should rise again; and as He lives a new life in heaven, so we *should walk in newness of life*. This, says the apostle, our very baptism represents to us. [Romans 6:4]

Therefore leaving the principles of the doctrine of Christ – That is, saying no more of them at present. *Let us go on to perfection; not laying again the foundation of repentance from dead works* – From open sins, the very first thing to be insisted on. *And faith in God* – The very next point. So St. Paul in his very first sermon at Lystra (Acts xiv. 15), 'Turn from those vanities unto the living God.' And when they believed, they were to be baptized with the baptism, not of the Jews, or of John, but of Christ. [Hebrews 6:1]

(6) Baptism is administered to infants

The basis of this administration of baptism is made clear in the notes above at Matthew 28:19 and Romans 2:25. Other relevant notes include the following

To circumcise the child – That He might visibly be 'made under the law,' by a sacred rite which obliged Him to keep the whole law; as also that He might be owned to be the seed of Abraham, and might put an honour on the solemn dedication of children to God. [Luke 2:21. For meaning of "dedication," see next note.]

She was baptized, and her family – Who can believe that in so many families there was no infant? or, that the Jews, who were so long accustomed to circumcise their children, would not now devote them to God by baptism? [Acts16: 15]

In the use of the phrase "so many families", Wesley may have had in mind Acts 16:33 and 1 Corinthians 1:16. Also, in this note the phrase "devote them to God by baptism" indicates the meaning of "dedication" in the note on Luke 2:21, ie children are dedicated to God by baptism.

For the notes at Romans 2:25 and Romans 6:3–4, see above at (5). The promises made by Christian parents at the baptism of their children provide the means for them to enter into the death and the resurrection of the Lord Jesus, into newness of life. Thus, these two verses and the notes on them can be applied to infant baptism as truly as to believers' baptism.

(7) Baptism is not an absolute requirement

In John 3:5 Wesley comments: " . . . be baptized (wherever baptism can be had) as the outward sign and means of it". Wesley is speaking of the change which the Holy Spirit makes in believers (see above at (3)), and which is not tied to baptism (see above under (1) – Acts 10:47). The signs of the Holy Spirit's work in people can be seen before baptism.

(8) The mode of baptism is of little importance

Confessing their sins – Of their own accord; freely and openly. Such prodigious numbers could hardly be baptized by immerging their whole bodies under water; nor can we think they were provided with a change of raiment for it, which was scarce practicable for such multitudes. And yet they could not be immerged naked with modesty, nor in their wearing apparel with safety. It seems, therefore, that they stood in ranks on the edge of the river; and that John, passing along before them, cast water on their heads or faces; by which means he might baptize many thousands in a day. And this way most naturally signified Christ's baptizing them 'with the Holy Ghost and with fire,' which John spoke of, as prefigured by his baptizing with water; and which was eminently fulfilled when the Holy Ghost sat upon the disciples in the appearance of tongues, or flames of fire. [Matthew 3:6]

The above note is based on the assumption that the immersion of so many would not have been "practicable" at that time and place. The impracticable nature of total immersion at certain times and places is more relevant at Acts 10:48 and Acts 16:33.

The comments about clothing are probably irrelevant. The number of people who came to John may be a valid pointer to the mode of baptism.

> [By the circumcision of Christ] Which He wrought in you when you were as it were *buried with him in baptism* – The ancient manner of baptizing by immersion is as manifestly alluded to here, as the other manner of baptizing by sprinkling or pouring of water is, [at] Heb. x. 22. [Colossians 2:12]

> *Let us draw near* – To God. *With a true heart* – In godly sincerity. *Having our hearts sprinkled from an evil conscience* – So as to condemn us no longer. *And our bodies washed with pure water* – All our conversation [way of life] spotless and holy, which is far more acceptable to God than all the legal sprinklings and washings. [Hebrews 10:22]

Wesley has made his point about baptism by sprinkling in his cross-reference at Colossians 2:12 to Hebrews 10:22. Here he concentrates on the spiritual effects of baptism. Thus he demonstrates that the mode of baptism is a minor matter, even irrelevant. Wesley is showing the same attitude to the mode of baptism as Paul showed to the question of the person who baptises, at 1 Corinthians 1:17.

The sermon on the means of grace is in harmony with the notes quoted on the Sacraments of Baptism (above) and of Holy Communion (below).

Holy Communion

Wesley travelled perhaps 250,000 miles proclaiming the Gospel in England, Scotland, Wales and Ireland. He preached on thousands of occasions. The changes in people, and the groups into which Wesley banded them, ensured the growth and continuance of this evangelism. Evening prayer meetings extended into the hour past midnight. It was an exciting work. In this enthusiasm (in the Wesleyan sense of the word) the

Lord's Supper had a prominent place.

Wesley returned to Oxford University in 1729 and from that time regular attendance at Holy Communion became one of the rules of the Holy Club. His *Journal* from 1735 to1738 shows that he partook regularly of the sacrament on board ship and in the colony. After the religious experience of both John and Charles in May 1738, Holy Communion continued to be prominent in their devotional life, and in their teaching. On Sunday 1 April 1739 John attended three services – one at which George Whitefield preached, another at which he preached himself, and a society meeting with "singing etc.". He returned home for supper and then at "11 PM at Mr. Deschamps', thirty there, communion, prayer, singing". He returned home again at 1 am! One factor leading to the withdrawal of Wesley and his followers from the Fetter Lane Society, in July 1740, was the Lord's Supper. In the same year, from 1 June to 31 August, Wesley records eight services of communion on Sundays, and nine in peoples homes, with 30 present on one occasion. The *Journal* entries for 26–28 June 1740 show how important he considered Holy Communion to be for the members of the Methodist Societies: " . . . the Lord's Supper was ordained by God, to be a means of conveying to men either preventing, or justifying, or sanctifying grace". This is the same message as appears in the sermon on 'The Means of grace' (1746).

In 1745, seven years into the Evangelical Revival, the Wesley brothers published *Hymns on the Lord's Supper* – 166 of them! John Wesley ordained bishops for the work in America so that the Methodists might receive the Lord's Supper. In 1789 Wesley records 69 communions; in 1790, 54; and in 1791, 15 communions to mid-February. He died on 2 March. Throughout his ministry John Wesley kept together Word and Sacrament.

Wesley's understanding of the Lord's Supper is mostly to be found at 1 Corinthians 11:20–29. The following notes on these verses should be read with the Bible open at this point.

Therefore – That is, in consequence of those schisms [see verse 19]. *It is not eating the Lord's Supper* – That solemn memorial of His death; but quite another thing. [verse 20]

For in eating what you call the Lord's Supper, instead of all partaking of one bread, each person brings his own supper, and eats it without staying for the rest. And hereby the poor, who cannot provide for themselves, have nothing; while the rich eat and drink to the full: just as the heathens used to do at the feasts on their sacrifices. [verse 21]

Have ye not houses to eat and drink your common meals *in? or do ye despise the church of God?* – Of which the poor are both the larger and the better part. Do ye act thus in designed contempt of them? [verse 22]

I received – By an immediate revelation. [verse 23]

This is My body, which is broken for you – That is, this broken bread is the sign of My body, which is even now to be pierced and wounded for your iniquities. Take then, and eat of, this bread, in a humble, thankful, obediential remembrance of My dying love; of the extremity of My sufferings on your behalf, of the blessings I have thereby procured for you, and of the obligations to love and duty which I have by all this laid upon you. [verse 24]

After supper – Therefore ye ought not to confound this with a common meal. *Do this in remembrance of me* – The ancient sacrifices were in remembrance of sin: this sacrifice, once offered, is still represented in remembrance of the remission of sins. [verse 25]

Ye show forth the Lord's death – Ye proclaim, as it were, and openly avow it to God, and to the whole world. *Till he come* – In glory. [verse 26]

Whosoever shall eat this bread unworthily – That is, in an unworthy, irreverent manner; without regarding either Him that appointed it, or the design of its appointment. *Shall be guilty of* profaning that which represents *the body and the blood of the Lord.* [verse 27]

But let a man examine himself – Whether he know the nature and the design of the institution, and whether it be his own desire and purpose thoroughly to comply therewith. [verse 28]

For he that eateth and drinketh so unworthily as those Corinthians did, *eateth and drinketh judgement to himself* – Temporal judgements of various kinds (verse 30). *Not distinguishing* the sacred tokens of *the Lord's body* – From his common food. [verse 29]

From these notes, and others, Wesley's understanding of the Lord's Supper can be established.

(1) The Lord's Supper is a memorial

Wesley refers at 1 Corinthians 11:20 to that "solemn memorial"; at verse 24 to "a humble, thankful, obediential remembrance of My dying love"; and at verse 25 to the "remembrance of the remission of sins". Wesley's note at verse 26 contains the idea of memorial without the word. Relevant further notes include:

This is my blood of the new testament – That is, This I appoint to be a perpetual sign and memorial of My blood, as shed for establishing the new covenant; that all who shall believe in Me may receive all its gracious promises. [Mark 14:24]

With desire have I desired – That is, I have earnestly desired it. He desired it, both for the sake of His disciples, to whom He desired to manifest Himself further at this solemn parting; and for the sake of His whole Church, that He might institute the

121

grand memorial of His death. [Luke 22:15]

(2) The Lord's Supper is a sign of the death, which seals the new covenant

. . . this broken bread is the sign of My body . . . pierced and wounded for your iniquities. [1 Corinthians 11:24]

. . . this sacrifice, once offered, is still represented in remembrance of the remission of sins. [1 Corinthians 11:25]

The word "represented" is used at both verses 25 and 27. This word is used by Wesley in his preface to the *Hymns on the Lord's Supper*. His meaning when he uses the word may be conveyed in the following quotations from the preface:

[Jesus] was pleased at his Last Supper to ordain this [sacrament] as a Holy Memorial and Representation of what he was then about to suffer . . . This sacrament makes the thing which it represents, as really present for our use, as if it were newly done. The main intention of Christ herein (in this sacrament) was not, the bare Remembrance of His Passion; but over and above, to invite us to his Sacrifice; not as done and gone many years since, but as to grace and mercy still lasting, still the same as when it was first offered to us.

Further relevant notes include:

Jesus took the bread – The bread, or cake, which the master of the family used to divide among them, after they had eaten the Passover. This custom our Lord now transferred to a nobler use. *This* bread *is*, that is, signifies or represents, *my body*, according to the style of the sacred writers. Thus, Gen. xl. 12, 'The three branches are three days.' Thus, Gal. iv. 24, St. Paul, speaking of Sarah and Hagar, says, 'These are the two covenants.' Thus, in the grand type of our Lord, Exod. xii. 11, God says of the paschal lamb, 'This is the Lord's Passover.' Now Christ, substituting the Holy Communion for the Passover, follows the style of the Old Testament, and uses the same expressions the Jews were wont [accustomed] to use in celebrating the Passover. [Matthew 26:26]

This is the sign of My blood, whereby the new testament, or covenant, is confirmed. *Which is shed for many* – As many as spring from Adam. [Matthew 26:28]

For Mark 14:24, see (1) above.

And he took bread – Namely, some time after, when supper was ended, wherein they had eaten the paschal lamb. *This is my body* – As He had just now celebrated the paschal supper, which was called the Passover, so, in the like figurative language, He calls this bread His body. And this circumstance of itself was sufficient to prevent any mistake, as if this bread was His real body, any more than the Paschal lamb was really the Passover. [Luke 22:19]

This cup is the new testament – Here is an undeniable figure, whereby the cup is put for the wine in the cup. And this is called *the new testament* in Christ's *blood*, which could not possibly mean, that it was the new testament itself, but only the seal of it, and the sign of that blood which was shed to confirm it. [Luke 22:20]

(3) The Lord's Supper is central to the life of the Church

Take then, and eat of, this bread, in humble, thankful, obediential remembrance of My dying love . . . of My sufferings on your behalf, of the blessings . . . procured for you, and of the obligations to love and duty . . . laid upon you. [1 Corinthians 11:24]

And they continued steadfast – So their daily church communion consisted in these four particulars: (1) hearing the word; (2) having all things common; (3) receiving the Lord's Supper; (4) prayer. [**Acts 2:42** – By communion Wesley here means sustenance.]

Continuing daily – breaking the bread – In the Lord's Supper, as did many churches for some ages. *They partook of their food with gladness and singleness of heart* – They carried the same happy and holy temper through all their common actions; eating and working with the same spirit wherewith they prayed and received the Lord's Supper. [Acts 2:46]

As the introduction to the sacrament of the Lord's supper shows above, Wesley partook of Holy Communion often throughout his life, but not daily. There are weeks, even months, when the diary does not record 'communion'. This seems to indicate that to partake daily is the ideal, but this is not always possible. Even non-observance of both sacraments does not rule out the possibility that such a person may be a Christian, as the sermon on 'A Catholic Spirit' demonstrates. Nevertheless, in this sermon and in the *Notes*, Wesley affirms strongly the place of these two sacraments in the life of the Church.

Wesley's brief note at Acts 20:7 – "*And on the first day of the week, when we were met together to break bread* – That is, to celebrate the Lord's Supper" – makes clear that the first day of the week was the day for meeting together to receive the Lord's Supper.

The cup which we bless – By setting it apart to a sacred use, and solemnly invoking the blessing of God upon it. *Is it not the communion of the blood of Christ* – The means of our partaking of those invaluable benefits, which are the purchase of *the blood of Christ? The communion of the body of Christ* – The means of our partaking of those benefits which were purchased by *the body of Christ* – offered for us. [1 Corinthians 10:16]

We have all drunk of one Spirit – In that cup, received by faith, we all imbibed *one Spirit*, who first inspired, and still preserves, the life of God in our souls. [1 Corinthians 12:13]

(4) The Lord's Supper is a means of unity.

For it is this communion which makes us all one. *We being many are* yet, as it were, but different parts of *one* and the same broken *bread*, which we receive to unite us in *one body*. [1 Corinthians 10:17]

Is Wesley indicating a way by which Christians could/should become one without waiting for the resolution of differences concerning Holy Communion? We do this in memory of Jesus and in communion with Him, and He makes us one. This interpretation is supported by the note at Acts 11:17:

To us, when we believed – The sense is, Because we believed, not because we were circumcised, was the Holy Ghost given to us. *What was I* – A mere instrument in God's hand? They had inquired only concerning his 'eating with Gentiles.' He satisfies them likewise concerning his baptizing them; and shows that he had done right in going to Cornelius, not only by the command of God, but also by the event, the descent of the Holy Ghost. And who are we, that we should withstand God? particularly by laying down rules of Christian communion, which exclude any whom He has admitted into the Church of the first-born from worshipping God together. Oh that all church governors would consider how bold a usurpation this is on the authority of the supreme Lord of the Church! Oh that the sin of thus withstanding God may not be laid to the charge of those who, perhaps with a good intention, but in an over-fondness for their own forms, have done it, and are continually doing it!

(5) To partake of the Lord's Supper requires preparation on our part

And all ate the same manna, termed *spiritual meat*, as it was typical, (1) of Christ and His spiritual benefits; (2) of the sacred bread which we eat at His table. [1 Corinthians 10:3]

The wilderness experience of being fed by God is typical of (that is to say, points forward to) "Christ and His spiritual benefits". We invite people, in the service of Holy Communion to "feed upon Him in your hearts by faith with thanksgiving". He is "the sacred bread which we eat at His table".

And all drank the same spiritual drink – Typical of Christ, and of that cup which we drink. *For they drank out of the spiritual* or mysterious rock, the wonderful streams of *which followed them* in their several journeyings, for many years, through the wilderness. *And that rock was* a manifest type of *Christ* – The Rock of Eternity, from whom His people derive those streams of blessings which follow them through all this wilderness. [1 Corinthians 10:4]

Yet – Although they had so many tokens of the divine presence. *They were overthrown* – With the most terrible marks of His displeasure. [1 Corinthians 10:5]

Now these things were our examples – Showing what we are to expect if, enjoying the like benefits, we commit the like sins. [1 Corinthians 10:6]

For 1 Corinthians 11:20, see the above full text of the notes at 1 Corinthians 11: 20–29. Wesley's note on "those schisms" refers to divisions between Churches. It is equally relevant to divisions within a church.

At 1 Corinthians 11:25, Wesley warns "ye ought not to confound this with a common [ordinary] meal".

For 1 Corinthians 11:27, see the full note above. "Unworthily" means "in an unworthy, irreverent manner" without regard to Christ or to the purpose of the Lord's Supper, namely the remembrance of the death of Jesus for the forgiveness of sins. Some worshippers say: 'I'm not worthy to come to the table' meaning 'I'm not good enough.'

In his *Journal* for 28 June 1740, Wesley points out: " . . . every one who knows he is fit for hell, being just fit to come to Christ in this [way]".

For 1 Corinthians 11:28, see the full note above. Wesley has shown the "nature and design" of the Lord's Supper in these notes on 1 Corinthians 11:20–29.

(6) The Lord's Supper does not involve a miraculous change in the bread and wine.

For Luke 22:19–20, see the notes at (2) above. Wesley is thoroughly logical and thereby, simple to understand. The notes at these verses rule out any miraculous change in the bread and wine. This is not inconsistent with Wesley's use of the word "represented" and his view of the sacrament stated in the preface to the *Hymns on the Lord's Supper* – both are found at 1 Corinthians 11:25 under (2) above.

Wesley's prayer, added to Paul's at Hebrews 13:20, shows the Methodists for whom the *Notes* were written how they should partake of the Lord's Supper:

Now the God of peace, who brought again from the dead the great shepherd of the sheep, our Lord Jesus, by the blood of the everlasting covenant . . . By the application of that *blood*, by which this covenant was established, may He make you, in every respect, inwardly and outwardly holy!

Much more :–
Charles Wesley's
hymns on the
Lord's Supper —
See my book &
Summary.

10

Experimental Religion

Not again!

IN HIS *JOURNAL* OF 24 May 1738, Wesley recorded the following:

> In the evening I went very unwillingly to a society in Aldersgate-Street, where one was reading Luther's Preface to the Epistle to the Romans. About a quarter before nine, while he was describing the change which God works in the heart through faith in Christ, I felt my heart strangely warmed. I felt I did trust in Christ, Christ alone for salvation: And an assurance was give me, that he had taken away *my* sins, even *mine*, and saved *me* from the law of sin and death.

Wesley had at last experienced what he had sought for years – the forgiveness of his sins. Theologically he had known that Christ died for the sins of all; but how could one, he asked, have "a sense of forgiveness and not feel it"? On that evening of the 24 May 1738 Wesley felt forgiveness.

It is both interesting and worthwhile to note that in the next few days Wesley found much help in the daily services of the Church of England, and also in his private reading of the Bible, the same means of grace which he had used always. Ten days later he notes:

> All theses days I scarce remember to have opened the Testament, but upon some great and precious promise. And I saw more than ever, that the Gospel is in truth but one great promise, from the beginning of it to the end.

The experience of forgiveness changed his relationship to the Gospel. Religion was not primarily a matter of knowledge and obedience, but of acceptance of a promise – the promise of forgiveness to each who trusts in Christ, "Christ alone for salvation". Charles experienced the forgiveness of sins on the Sunday before John's experience. From that moment the two brothers "offered Christ" to all people. This life-changing experience Wesley expected of all preachers "in connexion with" him.

The *Notes on the New Testament* reflect this spiritual journey of John Wesley. The struggle to be a Christian by acts of devotion and duty, the awakening of fear in the face of death, the doubt of his acceptability to God, and also the peace and joy originating in the experience of forgiveness, all these appear throughout the *Notes* in challenges and appeals to the readers. "Lord, is it *my* case?" Wesley makes the reader ask him/herself (Matthew 7:23). In the parable of the unclean spirit returning to the clean but empty house, he challenges the reader: "Reader, is it thy case?" (Matthew 12:43). Because he is a servant of the Word, these challenges and appeals appear throughout the *Notes*, wherever the text allows. But some estimate of their cumulative effect may be obtained by reading such notes consecutively as they appear, for example at Matthew 1:17; 12:30, 32; 19:24; Luke 10:42; 16:26; Romans 8:9; and Ephesians 4:26.

The *Notes* present religion as a choice which people must make. To the statement of Jesus that Mary has chosen the good part, Wesley adds the briefest, and sharpest, of comments: "Reader, hast thou?" (Luke 10:42). Choice is necessary because "there are no neuters in this war" (Matthew 12:30). At Romans 8:9, he comments: "*If any man have not the Spirit of Christ* – Dwelling and governing in him. *He is none of His* – He is not . . . a Christian; not in a state of salvation." When such challenges and appeals strike home to the reader, he/she becomes "*heavy laden* – With the guilt and power of sin". For Wesley this means: "Believe in Me; receive me as your prophet, priest, and king" (Matthew 11:28 f). The meaning of these titles is made clear at Matthew 1:16.

Although the word 'experience' or 'experimental' does not appear at this note, it is implicit: to receive Christ who is also

God – see chapter 3, 'Christology' – this cannot be done without experiencing what is happening. The remainder of the note on Matthew 11:29 points to the experience of rest:

> *And ye shall find rest* – Whoever, therefore, does not find rest of soul is not meek and lowly. The fault is not in the yoke of Christ, but in thee, who hast not taken it upon thee.

This is the experienced result of the primary and fundamental experiencing Christ.

In the preface to the *Sermons*, Wesley claims that he is describing "the true, the scriptural, the experimental religion" (paragraph 6 – 'experimental' is the eighteenth-century equivalent for the current term 'experiential'). The phrase "experimental knowledge" occurs at Ephesians 4:13, Colossians 2:10 and 2 Peter 1:2. However necessary is the knowledge about Christ which is derived from Scripture and other sources – Wesley had such in abundance before May 1738 – this is incomplete until a person experiences forgiveness from Christ.

This idea, without the use of the word 'experimental', occurs in other notes. At Hebrews 6:11 Wesley comments that the full assurance of faith is "the highest degree of divine evidence that God is reconciled to *me* in the Son of His love"; and that the full assurance of hope is:

> . . . the same degree of divine evidence (wrought in the soul by the same immediate inspiration of the Holy Ghost) of persevering grace, and of eternal glory . . . But this assurance of faith and hope is not an opinion, not a bare construction of Scripture, but is given immediately by the power of the Holy Ghost; and what none can have for another, but for himself only.

At Hebrews 11:1 Wesley writes of "the divine supernatural *evidence* exhibited to . . . a believer". At Romans 3:28, justifying faith is described as that which "receives Christ".

Here is a living relationship between sinner and Saviour, an experience, a meeting. The note on the priority of justification to holiness (Romans 4:5) can scarcely be read without the reader feeling what Wesley is describing; there is an experiential element in it from the moment Wesley speaks of "the sinner . . . convinced of his sin and danger by the Spirit of God . . . trembling before the awful tribunal". A few lines later he writes of the person "who enjoys the manifestation of that pardon . . . earnestly pray that this happiness may be ours!" (Romans 4:7).

Various notes, along with the above, make clear that this experience is normal for believers:

The same Spirit beareth witness with our spirit – With the spirit of every true believer, by a testimony distinct from that of his own spirit, or the testimony of a good conscience. [Romans 8:16. See also Galatians 3:2, 14; Colossians 2:7, 12f; 1Timothy 5:12; and Hebrews 12:2.]

No note restricts the witness of the Spirit or experiential religion to particular kinds of Christians. The note on 2 Corinthians 13:5 is abundantly clear: "*Know ye not yourselves, that Jesus Christ is in you?* – All Christian believers know this, by the witness and by the fruit of His Spirit." (See also the note on Hebrews 6:4 f.)

Wesley's aim in the *Forty-four Sermons* was to make clear the "religion of the heart, the faith which worketh by love" (preface, paragraph 6). In the second sermon, 'The Almost Christian', Wesley proclaims at point II, paragraph 9:

The great question of all, then, still remains. Is the love of God shed abroad in your heart? . . . Do you desire nothing but Him? Are you happy in God? . . . And is this commandment written in you heart, 'That he who loveth God love his brother also'? Do you then love your neighbour as yourself? . . . as Christ loved you? Yea, dost thou believe that Christ loved thee, and gave Himself for thee? . . . Believest thou the Lamb of God hath taken away thy sins . . . And doth his Spirit bear witness with thy spirit, that thou art a child of God?

Thirty-seven of these sermons were published in the years 1746, 1748 and 1750. The *Notes*, completed five years later, contain the same connection between faith and love. At 1 Timothy 6:11, Wesley comments: "*Love* – This St. Paul intermixes with everything that is good . . . ". Faith is one of the good things listed in that verse. It is not a bare belief; it is clothed with love, which transforms it into a warm relationship. It is a "living faith" (James 2:24). The connection also appears in that faith is "the condition of acceptance" while "Love is salvation" (Romans 3:27; Luke 7:50). The note at Colossians 2:7 – "*Rooted in Him* – As the vine" – also implies a living relationship between the believer and Christ, as does the phrase "experimental knowledge of Christ". At 1 Timothy 2:15, the description "*in faith and love and holiness with sobriety*" Wesley paraphrases as "loving *faith* and holy wisdom". While this may not be justifiable exegesis, it demonstrates Wesley's conviction of the interpenetration of faith and love. Because believers have received "*the Spirit of adoption*" they cry to God "with desire, confidence, constancy" (Romans 8:15). Wesley derives every moment from a supernatural conviction that "Christ is a fountain of life in his inmost soul" – the Christ whom he says "loved me and gave Himself for me". Of this he has "divine evidence". There can be no appropriate response except a living, loving trust by the sinner, corresponding to the living, loving Saviour. Before May 1738, Wesley had true knowledge of religion and made the correct response by confessing sin and obeying the demands of his Lord. After 24 May, he had also "*the* living, experimental *knowledge of God*, our Father, Saviour, Sanctifier" (Colossians 1:10; see also Matthew 17:20).

Wesley's note on the Johannine assertion that "*God is love*" and his emphasis on experiential religion adds a new dimension to the legal and religious interpretation of the death of Jesus at

Romans 3:24–26. At 1 John 4:8 Wesley writes:

> God is often styled holy, righteous, wise; but not holiness, righteousness, or wisdom in the abstract, as He is said to be love: intimating that this is His darling, His reigning attribute, the attribute that sheds an amiable glory on all His other perfections.

While these other perfections point to an understanding of atonement in terms of justice and propitiation, such an understanding remains incomplete until God is felt as love. Judicial acquittal or sacrificial propitiation may be performed with a spiritual distance between God and worshipper; love requires direct contact, a spiritual 'closing' with God.

Peter says that Christians have tasted that the Lord is gracious. Wesley interprets this as "Sweetly and experimentally known" (1 Peter 2:3). Grace or love cannot be understood unless experienced. Wesley's emphasis on "experimental religion" was and is essential; it brought to the fore what was missing from the orthodoxy of much of English religion in the eighteenth century. One best ask why?

An important point is the continuing nature of experience in Wesley's understanding of Christianity. It is not a matter of intermittent experiences of God – one at the moment of forgiveness, another at the moment of receiving the Holy Spirit, others at moments of seeking guidance. At Galatians 2:20, Wesley testifies that Christ:

> . . . Is a fountain of life in my inmost soul, from which all my tempers, words, and actions flow . . . I derive every moment . . . from a divine evidence and conviction that 'He loved me and delivered up Himself for me.'

At Ephesians 4:13, Wesley speaks of:

> . . . an experimental knowledge of Christ as the Son of God.

[which continues] To a state of spiritual manhood both in understanding and strength . . . To that maturity of age and spiritual nature wherein we shall be filled with Christ, so that He will be all in all.

This same point of continuous experience of Christ rings forth from the note on Philippians 3:8: the "experimental *knowledge of Christ*, as *my Lord* . . . King . . . reigning in my heart".

CJ Abbey and JH Overton in *The English Church in the Eighteenth Century*, make the point that in this period "the inner experience of the divine, the immediate vision of spiritual realities, was condemned as unwholesome enthusiasm and unfounded superstition". How did Wesley avoid this danger while emphasising "the inner experience"?

Two disciplines, which Wesley had received from his mother in childhood, remained with him to the end of his life. Firstly, the discipline of time is seen in the diary entries – he accounts for each hour of the day. Secondly, the discipline of study is to the fore in his years in Oxford, as student and tutor and as leader of the Holy Club, in which the study of Scripture is pre-eminent. In his *Journal* for 17 January 1739, Wesley defines enthusiasm as "false, imaginary inspiration" and the proof of its falsity is that "it contradicts the Law and the Testimony". Scripture is supreme. (See preface to the *Notes*, paragraph 10.) This being acknowledged, Wesley points out in the preface, paragraph 11, that in Scripture:

An exact knowledge of the truth was accompanied, in the inspired writers, with an exactly regular series of arguments, a precise expression of their meaning, and a genuine vigour of suitable affections.

Other notes of significance include the following:

But in understanding be ye grown men – Knowing religion was not designed to destroy any of our natural faculties, but to exalt and improve them, our reason in particular. [1 Corinthians 14:20]

. . . a Christian acts in all things by the highest reason, from the mercy of God inferring his own duty. [Romans 12:1]

Similar notes are found at 1 Corinthians 14:19 and 32. Wesley's considerable powers of reason are evident in all his sermons; he asks incisive questions about the text, and offers logical exposition of its parts.

Wesley's knowledge of Scripture was fundamental in his ministry before 1738 and also in his interpretation of the experience of 24 May. He relied on this knowledge and his reasoning about it when doubts arose. (See *Journal*, 24 May 1738, paragraph 15, to 28 May.) Reason, Scripture and experience were bound together for him. Wesley also acknowledged "the tradition of the Church", particularly the learning and heart religion of the early Church Fathers. Böhler's plea to Wesley, recorded in his *Journal* of 18 February 1738 – "My brother, my brother, that philosophy of yours must be purged away" – pointed to the need to experience Christ. Philosophy, reason, even knowledge of the Scriptures are useless without the experience of Christ, without heart religion. But the experience must be in the context provided by Scripture and a correct understanding of it:

For these things of him [God] which are invisible, are seen – By the eye of the mind. Being understood – They are seen by them, and them only, who use their understanding. [Romans 1:20]

Wesley experienced God for himself, as this note indicates. He maintained this experience to the end of his life through the use of Scripture, reason and tradition. These kept his religious enthusiasm true to God and free of any falsity.

Perhaps it wasn't always so simple?

References to Scripture Texts
Preface: paragraph 10
Matthew: 1:17; 7:23; 11:28–29; 12:30, 32, 43; 17:20; 19:24
Luke: 7:50; 10:42; 16:26
Romans: 1:19–20; 3:24–28; 4:5; 8:9, 15–16
2 Corinthians: 3:5
Galatians: 2:20; 3:2, 14
Ephesians: 2:1, 5; 4:13, 26
Philippians: 3:8
Colossians: 1:10; 2:7, 10, 12–13
1 Timothy: 2:15; 5:12; 6:11
Hebrews: 6:4–5, 11; 8:10; 11:1; 12:2
James: 2:24
1 Peter: 2:3
2 Peter: 1:2
1 John: 4:8

11
Practical Christianity

IN THE *NOTES* THE ATTENTION of those who "have a sincere desire to save their souls" is drawn again and again to the expression of Christianity in their lives and its vital importance. One of the great divisions of eighteenth-century England was wealth. JH Plumb in his *England in the Eighteenth Century* writes of Wesley's "rabid envy of luxury and elegance, of the aristocratic and libertarian attitude of life" (p 97).[1] Is this comment justified?

Wesley is certainly correct to comment on "luxury and elegance, the aristocratic and libertarian attitude to life" on the basis of Scripture. Concerning the rich man who asked Jesus about eternal life (Matthew 19:16–24), Wesley comments that his "bosom-sin was love of the world", and adds that this may not be true of everyone who wishes to follow Christ. Nevertheless his comment on verse 24 is devastating: "Rich man, tremble! Feel the impossibility, else thou art lost for ever!" In the note on the disciples' question – *"Who then can be saved?"* – Wesley expresses his own feeling about the extremes of wealth and poverty in eighteenth-century England: "If rich men, with all their advantages, cannot, who? A poor man; a peasant; a beggar; ten thousand of them, sooner than one that is rich." Wesley is not expressing envy of the rich nor a preference for the conversion of the poor; he is stating a fact of experience. He goes on to emphasise that it is not impossible for God to save the rich (verse 26). Warning comments with regard to wealth are also made at Matthew 6:19, 24; 8:34; Luke 7:36; 14:12; 16:19–31; 19:23; Romans 13:13; Galatians 5:21; 1 Timothy 3:8; 5:8; 6:9–10; Hebrews 8:11; and James 2:1–7.

Wesley's warnings about wealth are sometimes very cutting, such as: "They loved their swine so much better than their souls." On the other hand, they are often balanced by notes of mercy and hope. However difficult it may be for a rich person

137

to be saved, it is not impossible with God, although it requires "the utmost effort" of God (Matthew 19:26). In Wesley's estimation the rich man's "damnable idolatry . . . was enough to sink him to the nethermost hell" and "a thousand apparitions cannot effect this [ie a change in the heart of such a person]: God only can, applying His word" (Luke 16:25, 31). Earlier, Wesley comments on the warning of Jesus to those who "*have not been faithful in the unrighteous mammon*"; he emphasises that the rich are stewards, not proprietors. He does not advocate sales of estates, because God "lodges them in your hands for a season; but still they are His property". Wesley drives home this meaning at Luke 16:12:

> Rich men, understand and consider this. If your steward uses any part of *your* estate . . . any further or any otherwise than you direct, he is a knave: he has neither conscience nor honour. Neither have you either one or the other, if you use any part of that estate which is in truth God's, not yours, any otherwise than He directs.

When people cease to trust in riches "which they may lose in an hour"[2] and trust rather "*in the living God*", they may enjoy all things including riches "As His gift". But Wesley adds immediately: "Where else is there any notice taken of the *rich*, in all the apostolic writings, save to denounce woes and vengeance upon them?" (1 Timothy 6:17). Wesley has no comment on the women who ministered to Jesus of "their substance" (Luke 8:3), but then, the *Notes* are "explanatory" and this needs no explanation; Wesley is a servant of the word. Wesley is concerned with riches and all that accompanies it as a barrier to living a truly Christian life. The note at James 5:4 may be read as a denunciation of the conditions of domestic service and industrial labour imposed by the rich.[3] Nevertheless, he recognises "The supreme law . . . which is love, and that to every man, poor as well as rich" (James 2:8).

With regard to elegance of dress of the rich, Wesley speaks

plainly. At 1 Timothy 2:9, Wesley refers to artificially curled hair and ornamental gold, "Jewels of any kind" and costly raiment:

> These four are expressly forbidden by name to all *women* (here is no exception) *professing godliness*; and no art of man can reconcile with the Christian profession the wilful violation of an express command.

Wesley repeats this prohibition at 1 Peter 3:3 and adds at verse 4:

> All superfluity of dress contributes more to pride and anger than is generally supposed . . . 'I do not *regard* these things,' is often said by those whose hearts are wrapped up in them: but offer to take them away, and you touch the very idol of their soul.

He does rather go on about it.

Wesley's insight into the result of extravagant dress is surely correct. It is typified in this comment on "*a certain rich man*" at Luke 16:19. (See also note on Romans 13:13.)

Besides notes of mercy and hope for the rich in the midst of the dangers of wealth, Wesley insists on the necessity for Christians to work and provide for themselves and their families. On Paul's advice to the Thessalonians that they should work with their hands, Wesley comments at 1 Thessalonians 4:11: "Not a needless caution; for temporal concerns are often a cross to them who are newly filled with the love of God". This is in order that they "*may want nothing*". Wesley explains at verse 12: "*And may want nothing* – Needful for life and godliness. What Christian desires more?" Wesley insists also on the necessity to use money correctly and to gain it correctly. For example, burning the books of the former magicians at Ephesus " was far better than selling them, even though the money had been given to the poor" (Acts 19:19). Further comments about earning and using money are to be found at 1 Timothy 5:8; Acts 2:45; 4:32; 5:3 f; Romans 15:26; 1 Corinthians 16:2; Ephesians

4:28; and Matthew 25:40.

The expression of anger, so common in the eighteenth century (see Fielding's novel[1]), receives Wesley's attention on the basis of Matthew 5:22: *He tells the Counties 4 / He use for reason!*

... Christ teaches that we ought not for any cause to be so angry as to call any man ... *Fool.* We ought not for any cause to be angry at the person of the sinner, but rather at his sin only. Happy world, were this plain and necessary distinction thoroughly understood, remembered, practised!

Wesley draws his readers' attention to the command to "*Let not the sun go down upon your wrath*", and drives his note home with the pointed question: "Reader, do you keep it?" (Ephesians 4:26; see also Matthew 12:19, 36 f; and Luke 16:25). The notes about forgiving someone who sins against you are equally challenging, at Matthew 18:15–17.

The *Notes*, as is to be expected, declare adultery and fornication to be "at all times evil" (1 Corinthians 6:13, also verses 17, 18; Matthew 5:29 f; Ephesians 5:3; and 1 Thessalonians 4:3–6). But, what was not expected in the eighteenth century[4] was mercy for such people, as in the note at Ephesians 4:26: "Anger at sin is not evil; but we should feel only pity to the sinner." (See also John 8:6–11 and Jude 22.)

Despite excessive drinking by rich and poor in eighteenth-century England,[5] Wesley comments strictly on the text at each place relating to this question, as at Ephesians 5:18, and sometimes not at all, as at 1 Timothy 3:3 and 5:23. His note concerning the disciples and drunkenness at Luke 21:34 draws attention to the "need to warn even strong Christians against the very grossest sins"; and to "such sins as these", without focussing on drunkenness. Wesley goes so far as to affirm that "our Lord allows wine; especially at a festival solemnity" (John 2:2; see also Matthew 22:5). Wesley is truly a servant of the word; he does not stretch the New Testament references to drunkenness to imply total abstinence.

It is at first surprising that the Notes contain only one comment about slavery, so large a part had it in eighteenth-century England.[6] The comment on Colossians 3:11 supplies a clue to the reason for this single reference:

> . . . it matters not what a man is externally [whatever contrasts society exhibits] . . . *But Christ is in all* that are thus renewed, *and* is *all* things in them and to them.

Wesley is correct here, to focus on the contrasts of society; these remain in society although they are of no consequence to those who are in Christ. Wesley makes no comment on the phrase "*slave nor free*", although he does comment on the other phrases of the verse (similarly at Galatians 3:28).

Wesley's comments on Ephesians 6:5–9 seem to presuppose acceptance of the current master/ servant relationship. However, he appeals to masters in particular to behave "with gentleness and humanity, not in a harsh or domineering way" and act not only according to contract but to go beyond it (Colossians 4:1; see also Colossians 3:22 f and Revelation 18:13). The notes on Philemon imply that Wesley approves the return of Onesimus to Philemon and the consequent renewal of the former master/ servant relationship, but now "*In the Lord* – As a fellow Christian" (verse 16). Whatever degree of slavery this relationship contained, it seems to have been more akin to the eighteenth-century master/servant relationship than to that century's slavery.

Wesley is correct to refrain from applying any of these texts to eighteenth-century slavery.[7] He is "*a workman that needeth not to be ashamed, rightly dividing the word of truth*" (2 Timothy 2:15).

At 1 Timothy 1:10 occurs the term "*manstealers*". Here Wesley speaks most vehemently against slavery and other forms of enforced labour:

Manstealers – The worst of all thieves, in comparison of whom highwaymen and housebreakers are innocent. What then are most traders in negroes, procurers of servants for America, and all who list soldiers by lies, tricks, or enticements?

However much Wesley dislikes slavery,[8] he remains a true commentator on the New Testament; he does not use the text for his own purpose. Nevertheless, this comment on "*manstealers*" and other comments quoted above are sufficient to outlaw slavery for Christians.

The *Notes* seem to offer no direct comment on the brutality of the eighteenth century. Of the crucifixion, Wesley gives a factual rather than an emotional description, and that only once, at Matthew 27:26. He makes no comment on the references to scourging and whipping throughout the New Testament, presumably because whipping, being a public spectacle, needs no 'explanatory notes'. However, the character of a Christian, described below, has no place for such brutality.

The importance of Christian virtues is seen by the care which Wesley takes to make clear the meaning of 2 Peter 1:5–7, adding to your faith courage and to courage etc: " . . . each preceding grace leads to the following; each following, tempers and perfects the preceding". Wesley defines temperance as "the voluntary abstaining from all pleasure which does not lead to God". It is to use the things of the world as:

> . . . a scaling ladder to ascend to what is above. Intemperance is to abuse the world. He that uses anything below, looking no higher, and getting no further, is intemperate. He that uses the creature only so as to attain to more of the Creator, is alone temperate, and walks as Christ Himself walked.

This is fully harmonious with Wesley's comments on wealth, for example at Luke 16:12. Godliness is not the crown of the virtues; it must lead to brotherly kindness which "tempers and perfects" it; otherwise it may be "sour godliness" and "is of the devil". The crown of the virtues is love – "the pure and perfect love of God and of all mankind" (2 Peter 1:5–7). The supremacy of love appears also in the note on 1 Corinthians 13: "The necessity of love is shown, verses 1–3. The nature and properties, verses 4–7. The duration of it, verses 8–13". Wesley's general description of love in the note to verse 4 is worth quoting at length:

> The love of God, and of our neighbour for God's sake, is patient toward all men. It suffers all the weakness, ignorance, errors, and infirmities of the children of God; all the malice and wickedness of the children of the world: and all this, not only for a time, but to the end. And in every step toward overcoming evil with good, it is kind, soft, mild, benign. It inspires the sufferer at once with the most amiable sweetness, and the most fervent and tender affection.

Wesley concludes: "*Faith, hope, love* – Are the sum of perfection on earth . . . " (verse 13). (See also the notes on Matthew 5:48; 25:4 and Mark 12:29–31.) Wesley's comment at Galatians 5:14 – "*For all the law is fulfilled in this; Thou shalt love thy neighbour as thyself* [shows remarkable psychological insight] – Inasmuch as none can do this without loving God (I John iv. 12) . . .". Our love of God is needful to sustain our love for "the children of God" in the face of their "weakness, ignorance, errors and infirmities" towards us, and also our love for "the children of the world" in the face of their "malice and wickedness" (1 Corinthians 13:4). For Wesley, the "*love* of God contains the whole of Christian perfection, and connects all the parts of it together",[9] a very apt paraphrase of "*the bond of perfection*" of Colossians 3:14. The following verse proclaims the "*reward*" of such love – the peace of God shall "sway every temper, affection, thought". For Wesley, love is supreme in every aspect of the Christian's life, *"the glorious spring of all inward and outward holiness" (1 Timothy 6:10*; see also Matthew 12:7).

Opposite to this picture are two types of people – "workers of

143

iniquity" and "honest, inoffensive, good sort of people" (note at head of Matthew 25). Jesus had before declared what would be the portion of the former, for example the hypocrites (Matthew 24:51); those who despise others (Matthew 5:22); and those who work iniquity (Matthew 7:23). Wesley interprets Matthew 25 as applying to the second type of people, "honest, inoffensive, good". He asks: "But what will become of those who do no harm? . . . We have a clear and full answer to this important question." In his notes, Wesley interprets verses 3–9, about those who gained entrance and those for whom the door was shut; he has no comment on verses 10–12. If the meaning of verses 3–9 is made clear, the result of preparation or the lack of preparation is abundantly clear in the text (verses 10–12). The foolish, to whom the door is shut, are living on past experience of God; the wise "daily sought a fresh supply of spiritual strength, till their faith was made perfect" (verse 4). The foolish have "none to supply their future want" (verse 3). They are harmless, but they are shut out of heaven.

At verse 14 Wesley declares: "Our Lord proceeds by a parable still plainer (if that can be) to declare the final reward of a harmless man." The notes here focus on the man who received one talent and spotlight the fact, in verse 30, that he did no harm: " . . . for barely doing no harm, he is consigned to outer darkness . . . So mere harmlessness, on which many build their hope of salvation, was the cause of his damnation!". Two lines later Wesley reaches the answer to his opening question: "The same great truth, that there is no such thing as negative goodness, is in this chapter shown three times." Those "who do no harm" will go "*into the everlasting fire . . . prepared for the devil and his angels*". Wesley comments at verse 41, with a twinge of regret: "Not originally [prepared] for you; you are intruders into everlasting fire." Regretfully this is the final state of these harmless people (see note on verse 46).

Perfection, Wesley sees as the final goal of the Christian, and the criterion of the Christian character (Matthew 7:21). This is not a fixed criterion, something static. The wise who were admitted to the feast of their bridegroom "daily sought a fresh supply of spiritual strength, till their faith was made perfect". (Matthew 25:4). On the command to watch, Wesley writes at Matthew 25:13: "He that watches not only has a burning lamp, but likewise oil in his vessel. And even when he sleepeth his heart waketh. He is quiet, but not secure." Wesley's meaning seems to be that the wise Christian has love (equals oil – see verse 4) in reserve for any unforeseen situation. He can sleep at peace, but always his mind is watchful for Christ. He is quiet but not in the sense that he is sure of ultimate salvation; the perfection of that moment will not suffice for all future moments. The same continuing nature of perfection is implicit in the notes on the two great commandments, at Mark 12:30–33: to love God with "the whole strength and capacity of thy understanding, will, and affections" should develop as these three develop. At the Lucan parallel (10:27), Wesley directs attention to service, as is appropriate in that context (of the Good Samaritan). Such service has no limit except capability, and no termination except death. The command of Christ that the apostles should love one another is "new as to the degree of it, *as I have loved you*" (John 13:34). That degree is explained in part by verse 1 and the note thereon: "*Loved them to the end* – Of His life*". Perfection, which is love, cannot be static; for every situation of life requires a fresh and different expression of love, and requires this to the end of life. Christians are to be " . . . *filled* . . . *With all the fulness of God* – With all His light, love, wisdom, holiness, power, and glory. A perfection far beyond a bare freedom from sin" (Ephesians 3:19). Who could claim to be so filled in this life? (See also the note on Ephesians 4:24.) Wesley longs to be raised "into all the life of love" and to be "dead to all things here below" (Philippians 3:10).

This continuing growth of perfection Wesley expresses with beauty and clarity in a note on Philippians 3:12: "*Or am already perfected* – There is a difference between one that is perfect and one that is *perfected*. The one is fitted for the race (verse 15); the other, ready to receive the prize." He is not "already possessed of perfect holiness", but he is pursuing it "with the whole bent and vigour" of his soul (Philippians 3:13). Wesley warns in Hebrews 12:14: "The not following after *all* holiness is the direct way to fall into sin of every kind." Thus, the continuing pursuit of perfection is not optional for the Christian – it is essential for his ultimate salvation. (See also the notes on 2 Corinthians 7:1 and 2 Peter 3:18.) But while the goal is clear – all the nature of Christ – the expression of this nature may not be the same in every person. To sell all may be an absolute duty for some; for others "it would be an absolute sin" (Matthew 19:21). This goal, the desire to be perfect, is the mark of a real Christian.[10]

It is interesting that Wesley has no comment on the phrase "*Make you perfect*" (Hebrews 13:21) even though this so clearly supports his teaching concerning Christian perfection. The reason seems to be that there is no need to "assist serious persons . . . in understanding the New Testament" at this point (preface, paragraph 1). The meaning is plain, for Wesley. He leaves Scripture to speak for itself.

For other comments on Christian character see notes at Matthew 25:25; Luke 10:28; Colossians 1:22; 3:12, 16; 1 Thessalonians 4:3; 1 Peter 2:5, 9; and 1 John 4:18–21.

This picture of the Christian character, of practical Christianity, is essential in a theological arrangement of the *Notes*. The Scriptures are the basis of doctrine and they contain much that concerns discipleship. If, as Wesley declares, the tree and its fruit "are both good or both bad" (Matthew 12:33), then theology should produce the Christian character described above. In the New Testament there is nothing to suggest that doctrine was formulated before the proclamation of the message; the message and its consequences in changed lives were of supreme importance. If there are works unworthy of Christ, then it seems fair to conclude that the faith of such a person is incorrect. James clearly links the two at 2:14, which Wesley comments on at length in his notes. The same link can be seen in Paul's letters to the Romans, Galatians, Ephesians and Colossians, each of which begins with theology and leads to Christian character. Wesley makes the same point at 1 Thessalonians 2:14: "The same fruit, the same afflictions, and the same experience, at all times, and in all places, are an excellent criterion of evangelical truth."

At 1 Corinthians 6:9, he comments: " . . . we are never secure from the greatest sins till we guard against those which are thought the least; nor, indeed, till we think no sin is little, since every one is a step toward hell".

References

1 Demonstrated in Roy Porter's *English Society in the Eighteenth Century*, Pelican Social History of Britain, Pelican. Also embodied in Henry Fielding's novel *Tom Jones*, first published in 1749, and reprinted in Penguin Classics.

2 Roy Porter, p 256.

3 Ibid, pp 101 f, 104 f.

4 Ibid, pp 32, 151 f, 290 f.

5 Ibid, pp 33 f, 234 f.

6 Ibid, pp 151–3.

7 See EF Scott, *The Epistles to the Colossians, Philemon, and to the Ephesians*, Moffatt Commentaries, 1948, pp 99 f.

8 References to slavery begin (a) in the *Letters of John Wesley*, 1774 – there are eight from 1787 onwards to the Abolition Committee or members thereof; (b) in the *Journal* as early as 1736. However, Wesley's first sermon on the subject seems to have been as late as 1788.

9 The love of God means either (i) our love for God, as here, or (ii) God's love for us at Romans 5:5.

10 The note on Matthew 19:21 makes this clear.

References to Scripture Texts

Matthew 5:22, 29–30, 48; 6:19, 24; 7:21; 8:34; 12:19, 33; 19:16, 21, 24–26; 22:5; 23:25; 24:45; 25: preface, 3–9, 13–14, 25, 30, 40–1, 46;

27:26; 18:15–17 (These notes show how seriously Wesley takes the sin of quarrelling, whether this is between two people within their own Christian community, or between two denominations. See also the sermon on 'A Catholic Spirit.')

Mark: 12:29–31, 33

Luke: 7:36; 10:27–28; 14:12; 16:12–13, 19, 22, 25, 31; 19:23; 21:34

John: 2:2; 8:6–7, 9–11; 13:1, 34

Acts: 2:45; 4:32, 34; 5:3–4; 19:19

Romans: 13:13; 15:26

1 Corinthians: 6:13, 17–18; 13 (The notes on the whole chapter show the central position which love has in practical Christianity.); 16:2

2 Corinthians: 17:1

Galatians: 3:8; 5:14, 21

Ephesians: 3:19; 4:24, 26, 28; 5:3, 18; 6:5–9

Philippians: 3:10, 12–15

Colossians: 1:22; 3:11–16, 22–23; 4:1

1 Thessalonians: 2:14; 4:3–6, 11–12

1 Timothy: 1:10; 2:9; 3:8; 5:8; 6:9–10, 17

Philemon: 16

Hebrews: 8:11; 12:14

James: 2:1–8, 14

1 Peter: 2:5, 9; 3:3–4

2 Peter: 1:5–7; 3:18

1 John: 4:18–21

Jude: 22

12
The Christian Hope

THE TITLE OF THIS CHAPTER has been deliberately chosen (following John Lawson) to reflect the hope Christians have concerning life after death. This is in harmony with Wesley's aim stated in the preface: " . . . I write chiefly for plain, unlettered men, who . . . reverence and love the Word of God and have a desire to save their souls" (paragraph 3). The *Notes* are directed to the reader: "Is this your case?" Religion is personal; it must be experienced if it is to be real (chapter 10). It will be lived if it is genuine (chapter 11). It seems fitting to conclude this doctrinal survey of the *Notes* with a summary of what the individual Christian may expect to experience when life on earth comes to an end. Some attention is given to wrath and hell, but the summary focuses mainly on the Christian hope.

(a) The Christian hope is of resurrection

At the end of the genealogy of Jesus, Wesley comments on the brevity of life.

> Thus are we likewise passing away! and thus shall we shortly be forgotten! Happy are we, if, while we are forgotten by men, we are remembered by God! if our names, lost on earth, are at length found written in the book of life. [Matthew 1:17]

For Wesley this is the Christian hope and it is definite, and often in his thoughts: "*Happy are the poor in spirit: for theirs is the kingdom of heaven* . . . the eternal kingdom, if they endure to the end" (Matthew 5:3); "*Happy are the meek: for they shall inherit the earth* . . . They shall enjoy whatever portion God hath given them here, and shall hereafter possess the new earth" (Matthew 5:5); "*Happy are the pure in heart: for they shall see*

God . . . In all things here; hereafter in glory" (Matthew 5:8). At Matthew 6:10, Wesley writes:

> *Thy Kingdom come* . . . May all mankind, receiving Thee, O Christ, for their King . . . be filled with righteousness and peace and joy, with holiness and happiness, till they are removed hence into Thy Kingdom of glory, to reign with Thee for ever and ever.

At Matthew 6:11, Wesley comments:

> *Give us*, O Father . . . *this day* . . . *our daily bread* – All things needful for our souls and bodies; not only 'the meat that perisheth,' but the sacramental bread, and Thy grace, the food 'which endureth to everlasting life.'

Further relevant references include: " . . . shut out from the feast; from grace here, and hereafter from glory" (Matthew 8:11); and *"One is taken* – Into God's immediate protection" (Matthew 24:40).

These and nine other references in Matthew alone demonstrate how prominent in Wesley's mind is the Christian hope of eternal life. Some of the notes in Matthew are direct exposition of a verse; others go beyond direct exposition, as at Matthew 6:11. Other references to the future life are found at Matthew 10:29–30; 10:39; 16:26; 18:3; 19:17; 20:23; 25:8; 26:29; 27:52–53; Acts 20:32; Romans 13:11; 1 Corinthians 1:18; Ephesians 4:4; 6:17; and 2 Timothy 4:18.

As Wesley says at 1 Timothy 1:17: "How unspeakably sweet is the thought of eternity to believers!"

(b) Assurance of the future life rests on the resurrection of Jesus

The resurrection of Jesus is "a pledge of ours" (1 Peter 1:3). He is "the original fountain of *eternal life*" (1 John 5:20).At 1 Corinthians 15:20, Wesley comments:

. . . [Paul's] proof of the Resurrection lies in a narrow compass (verses 12–19). Almost all the rest of the chapter is taken up in illustrating, vindicating, and applying it. The proof is short, but solid and convincing, that which arose from Christ's resurrection. Now this not only proved a resurrection possible, but, as it proved Him to be a divine teacher, proved the certainty of a general resurrection, which He so expressly taught. [He is] *The firstfruit of them that slept* – The earnest, pledge, and insurance of their resurrection who slept in Him . . .

At Matthew 27:52–53 Wesley speaks of *"coming out of the tombs after his resurrection went into the holy city . . .* God hereby signifying that Christ had conquered death, and would raise all His saints in due season". At 1 Peter 1:21, he indicates that Christians through Christ believe in God who raised Jesus from the dead. All our faith and hope proceed from the power of His resurrection. Further references to this assurance are found at the following: Mark 8:8; Acts 26:6; Romans 1:4; 1 Corinthians 15:22; 15:51; Colossians 1:18; 1 Timothy 3:16; 2 Timothy 1:10; Hebrews 4:13–14; 1 Peter 1:3 1 John 5:11, 13; and Jude 21 and 24.

(c) The resurrection hope is central to the present life

Wesley brings out the importance of this hope for our present life in the notes on 1 Corinthians 7:29–33:

The time of our abode here *is short*. It plainly follows, *that even they who have wives* be as serious, zealous, active, dead to the world, as devoted to God, as holy in all manner of conversation [behaviour], *as if they had none* – By so easy a transition does the apostle slide from everything else to the one thing needful; and, forgetting whatever is temporal, is swallowed up in eternity. [verse 29]

They that buy as if they possessed not – Knowing themselves to be only stewards, not proprietors. [verse 30]

And they that use this world, as not abusing it – Not seeking happiness in it, but in God: using everything therein only in such a manner and degree as most tends to the knowledge and love of God. *For the* whole scheme and *fashion of this world . . . passeth away*; in this moment flying off like a shadow. [verse 31]

The unmarried man – If he understand and use the advantage he enjoys – *Careth* only *for the things of the Lord, how he may please the Lord.* [verse 32]

But the married careth for the things of the world – And it is his duty so to do, so far as becomes a Christian. *How he may please his wife* – And provide all things needful for her and his family. [verse 33]

Wesley slides easily from everything else to the one thing needful. Everything "is swallowed up in eternity". The future life is not only certain, in Wesley's thinking; it is also central in determining actions and attitudes:

There is but one God . . . From whom are all things . . . And we for him – The end of all we are, have, and do. [1 Corinthians 8:6]

. . . your labour is not in vain in the Lord – Whatever ye do for His sake shall have its full reward in that day. [1 Corinthians 15:58]

And God is able to make all grace abound toward you . . . That ye may abound to every good work – God gives us everything, that we may do good therewith, and so receive more blessings. All things in this life, even rewards, are, to the faithful, seeds in order to a future harvest. [2 Corinthians 9:8]

In whom [Christ] *we have redemption . . . forgiveness* is the beginning of redemption, as the resurrection is the completion of it. [Colossians 1:14]

Oh, give me one thing – a safe and ready passage to my own country! [1 Timothy 6:7]

These quotations and the numerous references below show how important for Wesley is the connection between the future life and the present. See Matthew 12:37; Mark 10:38, 40; Luke 10:28; 12:21; 16:12; John 5:29; 12:50; 14:19;15:16; Acts 16:28; 26:18; Romans 7:10; 8:13; 8:37–8; 1 Corinthians 3:8; 2 Corinthians 1:6; 4:10; 7:10; 13:4; Galatians 2:20; 4:26; 5:25; 6:8; Ephesians 1:3, 19; 4:30; 6:17; Philippians 1:6; Colossians 1:27; 2 Timothy 2:4, 19; Titus 1:2; 3:5, 8; Hebrews 6:11, 18–19; James 1:12; 1 Peter 1:9, 11, 21–22; 3:7, 15; 1 Peter 4:13 – full reasoning for this affirmation is to be found in the notes at verses 14, 16, 19; 2 Peter 1:8–12.

(d) The nature of the future life

Wesley does not speculate on this matter; he simply comments on the Scriptures which refer to it. These comments relate to three aspects of the future life.

(i) With what kind of body do the dead come?

The question is as old as the Church of the first century (1 Corinthians 15:35). Paul's answer is given in the form of a parable – seeds of grain die and then new life comes:

. . . Death is so far from hindering life, that it necessarily goes before it. [verse 36]

Thou sowest not the body that shall be – Produced from the seed committed to the ground, *but a bare*, naked *grain*, widely different from that which will afterward rise out of the earth. [verse 37]

But God – Not thou, O man, not the grain itself, *giveth it a body as it hath pleased Him . . . and to each of the seeds . . . its own body . . .* proper to that individual, and arising out of the substance of that very grain. [verse 38]

So also is the resurrection of the dead – So great is the difference between the body which fell, and that which rises. *It* [the dead body] *is sown* – A beautiful word; committed, as seed, to the ground. *In corruption* – Just ready to putrefy, and, by various degrees of corruption and decay, to return to the dust from whence it came. *It is raised in incorruption* – Utterly incapable of either dissolution or decay. [verse 42]

It is sown in dishonour – Shocking to those who loved it best: human nature in disgrace! *It is raised in glory* – Clothed with robes of light, fit for those whom the King of heaven delights to honour. *It is sown in weakness* – Deprived even of that feeble strength which it once enjoyed. *It is raised in power* – Endued with vigour, strength, and activity, such as we cannot now conceive. [verse 43]

It is sown in this world *a* merely *animal body . . .* but *it is raised* of a more refined contexture, needing none of these animal refreshments, and endued with qualities of a spiritual nature, like the angels of God. [verse 44]

As Adam was the first general representative of men, Christ was the second and the last. And what they severally [each] did, terminated not in themselves, but affected all whom they represented. [verse 47]

At verse 40, Wesley asserts that we shall also bear the image of the heavenly.

Wesley's point is that Christ is representative of all who trust in him. They will have a body like Jesus had in the resurrection days – spiritual and recognisable, but now suitable to the life in heaven. Amen to this!

At Philippians 3:21, he writes that the Lord Jesus Christ will transform our vile body that it may be fashioned "*like unto his glorious body* – Like that wonderfully glorious body which He wears in His heavenly kingdom . . .".

Other references to the nature of the resurrection body are found at Mark 12:27, 35; 1 Corinthians 2:7; 2 Corinthians 5:1–4; 1 Peter 1:4; and 1 John 3:2.

(ii) Knowledge in the Next Life.

Wesley makes a strange comment at Luke 16:23, in the parable of the rich man who ignored the poor man: "*He seeth Abraham afar off* – And yet knew him at that distance. And shall not Abraham's children, when they are together in paradise, know each other?" This comment shows that Wesley is quite sure that we will know each other in heaven. His notes quoted in (i) imply the power of recognition and much more knowledge. We will have "a body endued with vigour, strength, and activity, such as we cannot now conceive". We expect the Lord Jesus to welcome us into heaven. We will be given "a body like unto His glorious body". In this assurance the note at Luke 16:9 is both justified and meaningful: " . . . when this earthly tabernacle is dissolved, those of them who have gone before *may receive*, may welcome, *you into the heavenly habitations*". (See also 2 Timothy 1:3: "One who stands on the verge of life . . .".)

The same transformation of our powers of knowing is affirmed at 1 Corinthians 13:10–12:

But when that which is perfect is come . . . In our present state we are mere infants in point of knowledge, compared to what we shall be hereafter . . . *then I shall know* . . . In a clear, full, comprehensive manner; in some measure like God [knows] . . .

One language shall prevail [be in general use] among all the inhabitants of heaven. [verse 8]

We shall be sure both of knowing one another and of understanding much that is not understandable now. We will know God and other believers.

(iii) What will we do in heaven?

> . . . *I shall know* . . . In a clear, full, comprehensive manner, in some measure like God . . . [1 Corinthians 13:12]

In the notes on the resurrection body given to believers (1 Corinthians 15:42–45), Wesley implies that this change is instantaneous: "*In a moment* – Amazing work of omnipotence!" (verse 52). However, on at least five occasions he also warns against applying the language of earth to the affairs of heaven. For example, at Romans 5:9, he states: "But wrath in God is not a human passion; nor is love, as it is in God. Therefore the inspired writers ascribe both the one and the other to God only in an analogical sense." The other occasions concerned are at Romans 8:28 (the sentence beginning "Whereas, to take this consulting . . . "; John 11:11; and Revelation 5:1; 7:15).

Thus the concepts of instantaneous events and events in a time sequence – concepts which are tied to the things of earth – may not be mutually exclusive when used in the context of the resurrection life. It may be possible that the knowledge which believers will be given (see (ii) above) will require something like time to be absorbed and to be appreciated, time in the sense of mental growth. We will be occupied in appreciating what it means to know and to love God as He knows and loves us.

Believers, in the resurrection life, shall "serve God" (Revelation 7:15). The AV uses this word at Revelation 22:3. Wesley translates "worship". He is confirmed in this alteration by the New RSV, REB, GNB, and JB. The meaning of "serve" is made clear in a note at Jude verse 1: "*Jude, a servant of Jesus Christ*".

This is the highest glory which any, either angel or man, can aspire to. The word servant, under the old covenant, was adapted to the spirit of fear and bondage that clave to that dispensation. But when the time appointed of the Father was come, for the sending of His Son to redeem them, they were under the law, the word servant (used by the apostles concerning themselves and all the children of God) signifying one who, having the Spirit of adoption, is made free by the Son of God. His being a servant is the fruit and perfection of his being a son. And whenever the throne of God and of the Lamb shall be in the New Jerusalem, then it will be indeed that "*his servants . . . Shall worship him*" (Revelation 22:3). Here Wesley explains "*Shall worship him* – The noblest employment."

When we know God in a "clear, full, comprehensive manner" (1 Corinthians 13:12), we will appreciate, more than we can possibly do with our present limitations, what God has done for us. We will know the love of God then, love which cannot be fully known now (Ephesians 3:19). With this appreciation and knowledge of God, we will worship Him beyond any worship offered on earth.

Another form of service is hidden in the word "*reign*" (Revelation 22:5) and implied in the parable at Matthew 25:14:30 (also Luke 11:24):

And they shall reign – But who are the subjects of these kings? The other inhabitants of the new earth. For there must needs be an everlasting difference between those who when on earth excelled in virtue, and those comparatively slothful and unprofitable servants who were just saved as by fire. [Revelation 22:4]

The Greek word reign and the word king have the same root. Wesley is correct to write "these kings".

Wesley's note is an honest attempt to explain "*they shall reign*". (Matthew Henry's attempt confuses the two Greek words – service of worship, and service of reigning.) But what foundation has Wesley for his claim that "there must needs be an everlasting difference" between Christians in the next life? At 1 Corinthians 3:12–15, Wesley affirms that in as much as Christians build on the only foundation, even though they build "doctrines, ceremonies, and forms of human invention", they

157

will be saved in the day of judgement. Nevertheless, they shall suffer loss – " The loss of that peculiar glory" which those who have built well will receive. At 1 Corinthians 15, Paul's account of the resurrection body of a believer allows for some difference. God gives each seed a body "proper to that individual" (verse 38). Nevertheless, at verses 42–44, neither Paul nor Wesley allow for any difference in the spiritual nature of the new body: " . . . *raised in corruption . . . in glory . . . in power* . . . endued with qualities of a spiritual nature . . .". Wesley notes at verse 52: "[All will be changed] *In a moment* – Amazing work of omnipotence! And cannot the same power now change us into saints in a moment?"

This rhetorical question is addressed to believers on earth. Wesley is certain that we can be changed on earth. Why does he seem to deny that this can be the case in heaven?

Perhaps a combination of the ideas suggested above may point to a solution to this problem.

(1) While the change is instantaneous, the appreciation of the love and work of God, Father, Son and Holy Spirit requires mental time to be absorbed. This will be more difficult for believers who had concentrated on "doctrines of human invention" than for those who concentrated on "true and solid doctrines".

(2) Is Wesley's understanding of "*they shall reign*" correct? The Gospel is about the king who comes humbly to die at the hands of his enemies. Even in heaven, Jesus reigns as the Lamb (at Revelation 22:3 and 25 other places in this book). The believers who reign with the Lamb must do so as love suffering for others. If they rule in this way over those who have been saved as through fire, their love will cause them to suffer with those other believers, and to bring them closer to God who is love. This theological arrangement of Wesley's *Notes on the New Testament* is not the place to present the author's views on this item of our Methodist standards. But there seems to be a contradiction between the notes at 1 Corinthians 3:14–15 and Revelation 22:4 on the one hand, and those at 1 Corinthians

15:42–44 and 52 on the other hand. The above paragraphs on the word *"reign"* attempt to solve this contradiction, using Wesley's principles of interpreting Scripture by Scripture, and by reason.

At Matthew 25:21–23 and Luke 19:17–18, Wesley makes no comment on the new status and responsibility of the servants who were rewarded by the master on his return. He directs his note to those who do not serve their heavenly Master now: *"He . . . Went and hid his master's money –* Reader art thou doing the same? Art thou hiding the talent God hath lent thee?" (Matthew 25:18)

This is the whole purpose of the parable. It is not intended to arouse curiosity about heaven.

Three explanatory words at Acts 20:32 should satisfy every believer about the nature of the future life: *"And to give you an inheritance –* Of eternal glory. *Among all them that are sanctified . . .".*

For Wesley, Christians on earth are "waiting for God's salvation" and those in heaven "are gone to enjoy it" (Luke 2:38). Amen.

(e) When will the resurrection be?

Two answers to this question appear throughout the New Testament.

(1) The dead will be raised when the Lord Jesus comes to judge the world. Believers who have died before this are "asleep in Christ". In 1 Corinthians 15, the resurrection of Jesus is described as follows:

The firstfruit of them that slept – The earnest, pledge, and insurance of their resurrection . . . [verse 20]

Afterward – The whole harvest. At the same time the wicked shall rise also. [verse 23]

[Christians are] . . . longing for that glorious day, when, in the utmost extent of the expression, *death shall be swallowed up* for ever, and millions of voices, after the long silence of the grave, shall burst out at once into that triumphant song, *O death, where is thy sting?* [verse 58]   / How does that fit in the reflection?

See also Matthew 27:52–53 (very thoughtful); Romans 8:23; John 11:11; Luke 23:43 ("*In paradise* – The place where the souls of the righteous remain from death till the resurrection."); Luke 16:22; 1 Thessalonians 4:13; Hebrews 6:12; and John 11:24 ("*Martha said to him, I know that he shall rise again in the resurrection of the last day.*" No comment is made by Wesley but the reply of Jesus seems to point to the second answer.)

(2) The resurrection of each believer is immediate, at death

To depart – Out of bonds [prison] . . . *And to be with Christ* – In a nearer and fuller union. It is better to depart; it is far better *to be with Christ*. [Philippians 1:23]

. . . *I give eternal life*. He does not say, I *will* give, but I *give*: for 'he that believeth *hath* everlasting life.' [John 10:27–9. This comment occurs in a sustained explanation of these three verses. It is strong support for the concept of immediate resurrection.]

He that believeth on the Son hath everlasting life – He hath it already. For he loves God; and love is the essence of heaven. [John 3:36]

I am the resurrection – Of the dead. *And the life* – Of the living. *He that believeth in me, though he die, yet shall he live* – In life everlasting. [John 11:25]

And where I am – In heaven [there shall also my servant be] . . . [John 12:26]

To know – By loving, holy faith. *Thee, the only true God . . . And*

Jesus Christ – As their Prophet, Priest, and King. *This is life eternal* – It is both the way to, and the essence of, everlasting happiness. [John 17:3]

Any idea of sleep between death and resurrection, or of paradise as a place where "the souls of the righteous remain from death till the resurrection" (Luke 23:43) seems to violate the idea of everlasting life which believers are given at the time of repentance and belief in Jesus. Any idea of paradise without Jesus (who is "in heaven" with God the father) seems to interrupt the union with the Lord which believers have on earth and will have in fuller measure after death. We are "waiting for God's salvation"; our ancestors in faith "are gone to enjoy it" (Luke 2:38).

Perhaps we will continue to find contradictions or ambiguities in the notes on the resurrection because we are using the language of earth, of time and space, for the affairs of heaven, where time and space do not exist as they do on earth – see above, subsection (d)(iii). Wesley explains the Scriptures which refer to the resurrection to the best of his ability according to the knowledge of his day. We "in the connexion established by Mr. Wesley" must explain them according to the knowledge of our day. Nevertheless, the certainty of the resurrection of believers, resting on the resurrection of Jesus, and the centrality of our resurrection for the shaping of our present life, require no further explanation in the present time than in Wesley's time. At John 14:1–6, Wesley affirms that there is a place in heaven for all who believe, even "a great multitude which no man can number" (verse 2). However, Jesus is *the way, and the truth, and the life* for believers now (verse 6).

Do the following references support (1) or (2)?: Acts 5:20; 11:14, 18; Romans 8:6; 2 Corinthians 5:8; and Hebrews 12:22–23.

(f) Jesus – His coming as Judge

In this theological summary of Wesley's *Explanatory Notes*, the connection between the resurrection of believers and their words and actions on earth has been made clear above, at section (c). Judgement will be made according to their words and actions and attitudes. The Judge is Jesus. His final coming is as Judge.

Our faith should not stop at His death, but be exercised further on His resurrection, kingdom, second coming. [Romans 8:34]

Ye may perhaps think that God does not so much regard your words. *But I say to you* – That not for blasphemous and profane words only, but *for every idle word which men shall speak* – For want [lack] of seriousness or caution, for every discourse which is not conducive to the glory of God, *they shall give account in the day of judgement*. [Matthew 12:36. For the significance of "so much", line 1, see verses 32 and 34.]

Your words as well as actions shall be produced in evidence for or against you, to prove whether you was [sic] a true believer or not. And according to that evidence you will either be acquitted or condemned in the great day. [Matthew 12:37]

With what majesty and grandeur does our Lord here speak of Himself! [Matthew 25:31]

Inherit the kingdom – Purchased by My blood, for all who have believed in Me, with the faith which wrought [worked] by love. [Matthew 25:34]

Inasmuch as you did it to one of the least of these my brethren, ye did it to me – What encouragement is here to assist the household of faith! But let us likewise remember to 'do good to all men.' [Matthew 25:40]

In his notes on the first kind of people in this parable, Wesley directs the reader's attention to faith and love (verse 34) and to works of outward mercy (verse 35). His notes on the second kind of people begin with a word of regret for their fate, at Matthew 25:41: "*Depart into the everlasting fire, which was prepared for the devil and his angels* – Not originally for you; you are intruders into everlasting fire."

In these notes on a few verses in Matthew, Wesley affirms the return of the Lord Jesus in glory, as judge of all at the general resurrection. He affirms judgement pronounced according to their faith in Jesus who died for their sins, and such faith shows itself in deeds of love. Forty references show how constantly this Christian hope was in the mind of Wesley: Matthew 10:28-42; 12:32; 16:27; 19:28; 21:44; 22:12; 24:29-46; 25:1, 8, 35; Mark 13:24, 32, 34; Luke 12:47, 58; 14:15; 19:13; 21:34; John 9:39; 16:11 (conclusion of note); 21:22; Acts 2:20; 3:21; 10:42; 17:3; 20:38; Romans 4:7; 6:23; 8:21-22; 1 Corinthians 3:13-15 (see note above at (d) (iii)); 15:24, 26; 2 Corinthians 5:20; Philippians 4:3; 1 Thessalonians 4:17; 2 Timothy 1:12; 4:8; Hebrews 9:27-28; 12:23; James 2:13; 5:8; and 2 Peter 3:10-13.

The six quotations below are representative of Wesley's pastoral concern in relation to judgement: Revelation

Waiting . . . For the glorious *revelation of our Lord Jesus Christ* – A sure mark of a true or false Christian, [is] to long for, or dread, this revelation. [1 Corinthians 1:7]

. . . 'He is long-suffering': He gives us space for repentance . . . [2 Peter 3:8. Verses 3-12 describe "the day of the Lord".]

Is it not lawful for me to do what I will with my own?–Yea, doubtless; to give either to Jew or Gentile a reward infinitely greater than he deserves. But can it be inferred from hence that it is lawful or possible for the merciful Father of spirits to 'Consign an unborn soul to hell, / Or damn him from his mother's womb'? *Is thine eye evil, because I am good?*– Art thou envious, because I am gracious? Here is an evident reference to that malignant aspect which is generally the attendant of a selfish and envious temper. [Matthew 20:15]

. . . judge nothing before the time – Appointed for judging all men. [1 Corinthians 4:5]

Immediately after the tribulation of those days – Here our Lord begins to speak of His last coming. But He speaks not so much in the language of man as of God, with whom a thousand years are as one day, one moment. Many of the primitive [first] Christians, not observing this, thought He would come immediately . . . [Matthew 24:29]

And I saw . . . In the right hand . . . It is scarce needful to observe, that there is not in heaven any real book of parchment or paper, or that Christ does not really stand there, in the shape of a lion or of a lamb. Neither is there on earth any monstrous beast . . . But as there is upon earth something which, in its kind, answers such a representation, so there are in heaven divine counsels and transactions answerable to these figurative expressions. [Revelation 5:1]

Wesley's pastoral concern shines clearly at another note, a seventh, to make these quotations complete:

. . . your names are written in heaven. Reader, so is thine, if thou art a true believer. God grant it may never be blotted out! [Luke 10:20]

He gives the Date as 1836!

(g) Wrath of God, and Hell

What place have the wrath of God and Hell in the doctrine of the Christian Hope; indeed, in the proclamation of the Good News? The second conference to which Wesley called his preachers (1745), discussed these two matters:

Q. Do not our assistants preach too much of the wrath of God and too little of the love of God?
A. We fear they have leaned to that extreme and hence some may have lost the joy of faith.
Q. Need we ever preach the terror of the Lord to those who

know they are accepted of him?

A. No. It is folly to do so, for love is to them the strongest of all motives.

At the conference of 1746, this subject was again discussed:

Q. What inconvenience is there in speaking much of the wrath of God and little of the love of God?

A. It generally hardens them that believe not, and discourages them that do.

Q. What sermons do we find to be attended with the greatest blessings?

A. 1. Such as are most close, convincing and practical.

2. Such as have most of Christ the Priest – the atonement.

3. Such as urge the heinousness of men living in contempt or ignorance of him.

This attitude to the proclamation of the bad news is reflected throughout the notes.

Ye know not what manner of spirit – The spirit of Christianity is. It is not a spirit of wrath and vengeance, but of peace and gentleness and love. [Luke 9:55]

Wesley acknowledges that Jesus spoke harshly to his enemies. But at Luke 13:32, he says:

But let us carefully distinguish between those things wherein Christ is our pattern, and those which were peculiar to His office. His extraordinary office justified Him in using that severity of language, when speaking of wicked princes and corrupt teachers, to which we have no call; and by which we should only bring scandal on religion, and ruin on ourselves, while we irritated rather than convinced or reformed those whom we so indecently rebuked.

Wesley is certain that there is wrath in God. He is equally

certain that it must not be understood in terms of "a human passion". We understand love in God by what he did and does for us, not in terms of "a human passion". We must try to understand wrath in God in terms of what God does. (See Romans 5:8-9; 1 John 4:8-10; and John 3:16-19.) Wesley may not supply this understanding of "wrath in God" in the *Notes on the New Testament*, but he clearly warns against an interpretation from a human point of view.

Other references to wrath occur in the notes at Matthew 27:46; Luke 22:44; Romans 4:15; 12:19; 1 Thessalonians 1:10; 5:9; and 2 Thessalonians 1:9.

The answers at those early conferences breathe the same spirit as the note at Matthew 25:41, which asserts that Hell "was prepared for the devil and his angels – Not originally for you; you are intruders into everlasting fire". Nevertheless, the note at Matthew 25:46 shows that Wesley is certain that "the punishment is strictly eternal". Who are the "intruders into everlasting fire"? The introduction to Matthew 25 supplies the answer:

> He [Our Lord] had before frequently declared what would be the portion of all the workers of iniquity [eg at Matthew 24:45–51]. But what will become of those who do no harm? honest, inoffensive, good sort of people? We have here a clear and full answer to this important question [in the three parables of Matthew 25].

Why do these people – the "workers of iniquity", people "who do no harm" – go to hell?

> . . . it is not the will of God that hinders [the seed to bear fruit in their lives], but their own voluntary perverseness. [Matthew 13:4. For examples of this perverseness see the notes at verses 19–21.]

> *Whosoever* . . . improves what he hath, uses the grace given

according to the design of the Giver . . . *But whosoever . . . improves it not – from him shall be taken* . . . Here is the grand rule of God's dealing with the children of men . . . [Matthew 13:12]

[With regard to the weeds among the wheat] . . . *An enemy hath done this* . . . with man's concurrence . . . [Matthew 13:28]

People go to hell as a result of their rejection of the way of God. Satan has a part in this rejection, but only with man's agreement. See also Romans 1:18.

Wesley's strong conviction about hell appears in the following notes:

But he that believeth not – Whether baptized or unbaptized, shall perish everlastingly. [Mark 16:16]

And the fire (either material or infinitely worse), that tormenteth the body, *is not quenched* for ever. [Mark 9:44]

Equally, Wesley has a strong conviction with regard to judging those who appear to be going to hell:

Father Abraham, have mercy on me . . . *But Abraham said, Son* – According to the flesh. Is it not worthy of observation, that Abraham will not revile even a damned soul? Shall living men revile one another? *Thou in thy lifetime receivedst thy good things* – Thou didst choose and accept of worldly things as *thy good*, thy happiness. And can any be at a loss to know why he was in torments? This damnable idolatry, had there been nothing more, was enough to sink him to the nethermost hell. *Besides this, there is a great gulf fixed* – Reader, to which side of it wilt thou go? [Luke 16:24–6]

This note brings out Wesley's strong pastoral concern for those who think they are going to heaven, but their damnable idolatry given to worldly goods and/or their judgmental attitude towards others indicates they are in great danger:

> . . . *the unclean spirit . . . Seeking rest, and findeth none* – How
> can he, while he carries with him his own hell? And is it not the
> case of his children too? Reader, is it thy case? [Matthew 12:43]

Wesley interprets Scripture in order to save people, not to condemn them.

Other references to hell occur at Matthew 5:22; 12:45; 19:24; 26:24; Mark 9:49-50; Luke 8:31; Acts 1:25; Romans 7:24; and Jude 5. *as CS Lewis pointed out mainly Dominical!*

References to notes on hell and wrath in the book of Revelation have not been included because Wesley confessed his despair of understanding this book, even after reading Bengel; see his preface to the Revelation in the *Notes on the New Testament*. His "short view of the whole contents of this book" shows, in the light of the nineteenth and twentieth centuries, how far he was from understanding this book.

Luther would have omitted it!

There is little mention yet (P15) Use of the Notes on the book of Revelation which denounce the Pope & Roman Catholicism and Herwick the date of the Lord's coming as 1836 which was challenged on #113 by Joseph Smith. Wesley was not altered the Notes. This was what Christopher Hopper meant when he talked about what Peake meant — Can out (1003) exegete, will what is said on P.113 really do "

Chapter 13
The Value of the Notes Today

THIS ARRANGEMENT OF *EXPLANATORY NOTES on the New Testament* focuses attention on what Methodist preachers are expected to believe and preach concerning these twelve doctrines. Looking at the notes as a whole, they also set preachers some general standards. Each of these is of value today.

(a) One of the distinctive features of the *Notes* is their origin. (see preface, paragraphs 7-8, and also Romans 8:28). Wesley, "a man of one book", as he claimed, evangelical and clear as he was concerning what he believed, learned from others. Bengel was a Lutheran, an academic, and, for the last 12 years of his life, a government appointee; Heylyn was a cleric of the Church of England which, at the time of the *Notes*, had closed many of its doors to Wesley, a cleric who spent all his ministry in a city church and was also a court chaplain. Both of these men served in forms of ministry very different from that which Wesley established for himself and his preachers. The congregations to whom they ministered directly were very different from the majority of people whom Wesley and his preachers touched. Nevertheless, Wesley drew from their commentaries; copiously from Bengel. The two other sources, Doddridge and Guyse, were dissenting ministers opposed to the Church of England in which Wesley remained a cleric to his death. They were also Calvinistic, with which view Wesley strongly disagreed. These sources of the *Notes* set us an example of accepting truth from others, however different they may be from us. For his Christian Library, established mainly for his preachers, Wesley used a wider variety of authors – Fathers of the early Church, medieval mystics, Puritans, Dissenting clergy, non-jurors, and Establishment churchmen. The truth of God comes to us from many directions.

(b) Wesley's attitude to Scripture is instructive. He had a very high regard for the Authorised Version. This does not use a capital letter for the personal pronouns referring to God (Father, Son and Holy Spirit). Wesley follows this custom scrupulously when he repeats the words of Scripture in his notes. But in his own words explaining the words of Scripture, he changes immediately to an initial capital. Another indication of his high regard for Scripture is seen in the format itself of the notes; the Scripture text is at the head of each page and in larger type than the notes themselves. (This is the format of the original editions.) Nevertheless, Wesley sought the best Greek text and dared to alter the Authorised Version on the basis of manuscript evidence provided by Bengel. How much more today should readers of the Bible seek the best translation, when codices and papyri of the Bible, discovered in the nineteenth and twentieth centuries, are numbered in thousands, and when commercial and private documents recently discovered, reveal the everyday usage of words in the New Testament. The *Notes* teach us to seek the original Greek words used by God's servants, and the true meaning of these in their context.

(c) Concerning the inspiration of the Scriptures, Wesley is certain that "In the language of the sacred writings . . . God speaks, not as a man, but as God" (preface, paragraph 12). Nevertheless, he does not jettison reason, as he remarks in a letter to Dr Rutherforth of 28 March 1768: "It is a fundamental principle with us that to renounce reason is to renounce religion." When this principle is applied to a particular Biblical passage, it requires the twentieth-century Christian to accept the results of geology, biology, astronomy and physics, and allows him to say, for example of Genesis 1–2, as Wesley says of Matthew 1: " . . . these accounts sufficiently answer the end for which they are recited. They unquestionably prove the grand point in view . . ." – in this case, that God created the universe, that man is the climax of that creation, and that he was made in God's image and given responsibility for God's creation. The Bible is to be understood from the point of view of its own purpose – namely, in Wesley's words in the preface to the Sermons: "God Himself has condescended to teach the way [to heaven] . . . He hath written it down in a book." This is the purpose of the Bible – to teach the way to heaven. For this purpose reason and religion go hand in hand.

(d) The *Notes* are on the New Testament, and on the whole of it. They do not omit the parts which Wesley did not understand, such as the Revelation. It is only too easy to concentrate on the parts of the Bible which are agreeable to us, either intellectually or emotionally or theologically, and to ignore the other parts. The *Notes* are a corrective to such bias, pointing to the completeness of teaching concerning the way to heaven. That way lies through the labyrinth of the human mind, the dangerous streets of the political city, the comfortable avenues of social life, and the open spaces of the universe. The Bible seen in the light of God's supreme revelation of Himself and His way, in the Lord Jesus, has much to say on all aspects of life. This respect for Scripture as applicable to all spheres of life is reinforced by the variety of the *Forty-four Standard Sermons*. These range over matters of faith and practice – from 'The New Birth' to 'The Use of Money,' from 'Salvation by Faith' to 'The Cure of Evil-Speaking.' The *Notes* as a standard of a Church remind its members that the Word of God applies to every aspect of life – to their thinking about God (Christian doctrine), to their experience of God (Christian experience), and to their living for God (Christian living).

(e) As a foundation document of the Methodist Church in Ireland and Great Britain, the *Notes on the New Testament* point to the supreme importance of the New Testament for Methodism. They set a standard concerning what is fundamental to the Gospel, and an objective of better understanding of the Scriptures, and both of these for the purpose of helping those "who have a desire to save their souls". But Wesley wrote the *Notes* to "assist serious persons . . . in understanding the New Testament", not to do it for them. Wesley's explanation must not be equated with Scripture, and neither should ours. Scripture is supreme. But its supremacy is meaningless without an understanding of it. Reason is required to interpret and apply Scripture. The reason should be one's own, but not in isolation; Wesley used other people's understanding of the Scriptures. This opens the door to differences of interpretation and application. Wesley differed from the Calvinists – Doddridge and Guyse – and even from his fellow Arminian, Bengel. Nevertheless, he respected them and learnt from them. Such differences must not be allowed to divide Christians. For Wesley, Scripture is crystal clear at certain places, for example, the commandments of the Lord Jesus. To the reply of Jesus to his questioner, at Luke 10:28, "*this do, and thou shalt live*", Wesley adds: "He, and he alone, shall live for ever, who thus loves God and his neighbour in the present life." If our differing understandings of Scripture cause us to part from other Christians and then to break this commandment, we have failed to understand Scripture. (See the sermon on 'Catholic Spirit.')

(f) The *Notes* were written for those who "desire to save their souls". They were written in the midst of an expanding evangelising and teaching movement, for both the evangelists and the evangelised. They set us a standard of interpreting Scripture, namely, so to proclaim the message of God in Christ that the hearers, in the words of Wesley's comment on the new birth, may "experience that great inward change by the Spirit" (John 3:5). They set us a standard of proclaiming this message with urgency. Every now and then the reader is directly addressed, as the teacher of the Law was by Jesus at Mark 12:34: " . . . *Thou art not far from the kingdom of God*", Wesley adding, "Reader, art not thou? Then go on: be a real Christian; else it had been better for thee to have been afar off." Urgency is necessary; there comes a moment when "the time is past and returns no more" (Matthew 25:9).

Postscript

IN A PUBLIC LECTURE IN Dublin University in 1983, Professor David Tracy stated: "Great developments of religious tradition were made in the search for spirituality, not in the attempt to counter error." The *Notes* bear witness to the truth of this claim. Where Wesley is only countering error, as in the notes relating to the Roman Catholic Church – this category includes most of the errors in the notes on Revelation – the *Notes* are of little value. But where he is countering with an opposing truth, the *Notes* are of great value, as when Wesley proposes the concept of grace, both prevenient and universal, to counter what he regarded as the Calvinist error (see chapter 5 'Grace').

The status of the *Notes* in the Methodist Church – namely, "to set up standards of preaching and belief which should secure loyalty to the fundamental truths of the Gospel of Redemption" (The Constitution, Section II) – is not vitiated by Wesley's errors in the notes on the Revelation, because the Gospel of Redemption does not depend upon the identity of the beast or the interpretation of its number, nor of any of the symbolism of this book. The Gospel was truly established in people's hearts and minds as well as committed to writing long before the Apocalypse.

The article on Hermeneutics in the *New Dictionary of Theology* (Inter-Varsity Press) includes a survey of this subject from the time of Schleiermacher to the present. Each school in this period recognises a fluidity of interpretation; the romanticists hold that "all interpretation is open to correction and revision". This article concludes:

> Biblical interpretation can never outgrow the work of the Biblical specialist. But neither can Biblical hermeneutics ever again be isolated from these broader yet fundamental inter-disciplinary questions.

The work of the Biblical specialist has advanced a long way since Wesley wrote the *Notes*. 'Wesleyans' need not be ashamed to acknowledge that their spiritual father was a child of his age in this respect.

In *The Analogical Imagination* (p 102), David Tracy states, in a discussion of the nature of a religious classic: "All understanding is mediational in the sense of happening now as I face the question mediated from the past and projected with hope to the future." In the *Explanatory Notes on the New Testament*, Wesley has fulfilled this description of understanding. He begins with the past, with the "word of God which remains for ever". Wesley faces "the question mediated from the past", his relationship with God, and the question "projected with hope to the future", how "to transcribe His life in our own" (preface, paragraph 9). These questions Wesley has answered for himself in the eighteenth century. His understanding of them is "mediational" in as much as it "assists" our understanding of the text and helps us to understand now "the question mediated from the past", our past which includes 200 years more than the past did for Wesley, and "the question projected with hope to the future", a future much more complex than eighteenth-century people ever imagined. By this test of a classic, the *Notes* belong to the religious classics.

Wesley, however, would probably be more than a little shocked by this estimation. To the lady who asked him about understanding God, he replied: "All you want to know of Him is contained in one book, the Bible. Therefore your one point is to understand this." Wesley saw the *Notes* as only assisting people in their thinking about God: the Word of God is supreme. If the *Explanatory Notes on the New Testament* point away from themselves to the Word of God, itself, and further, to the Word who is God, Himself, Wesley might accept that they are a classic.

Yes – a spiritual classic
but a 'standard' Now?
Have we Now to accept Wesley's
'Spin' on everything?

Index

a Very poor Index?